C000303086

QABALAH,
THE WESTERN
MYSTERY TRADITION

QABALAH, TAROT & THE WESTERN MYSTERY TRADITION

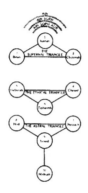

The 22 Connecting Paths on the Tree of Life

Compiled and Edited by
Clifford Bias

SAMUEL WEISER, INC.

York Beach, Maine

First published in 1997
by Samuel Weiser, Inc.
P.O. Box 612
York Beach, ME 03910-0612

Copyright © 1985 Clifford Bias
All rights reserved. No part of this publication may be reproduced
or transmitted in any form or by any means, electronic or
mechanical, including photocopying, recording, or by any infor-
mation storage and retrieval system, without permission in writing
from the publisher. Reviewers may quote brief passages.

Bias, Clifford.
   [Way back]
   Qabalah, tarot & the Western mystery tradition : the 22 connecting
paths on the tree of life / compiled and edited by Clifford Bias.
     p.   cm.
   Written by Clifford Bias.
   Originally published: The way back, 1985.
   Includes index.
   ISBN 1-57863-031-2 (pbk. : alk. paper)
   1. Cabala- -Miscellanea. 2. Tarot- -Miscellanea. 3. Occultism.
I. Title.
BF1611.B53   1997
133' .47- -dc21   97-29495
                                                    CIP

BJ

Typeset in 10 point Souvenir

Printed in the United States of America

04 03 02 01 99 98 97
10 9 8 7 6 5 4 3 2 1

The paper in this publication meets the minimum requirements of
the American National Standard Permanence of Paper for Printed
Library Materials Z39.48–1984.

Contents

List of Figures

Illustrations from the Tarot

The Tarot cards that illustrate the rituals in this book are from a deck called the Tarot Atu, given to the author many years ago by a Swiss gentleman. Bias tells us, "I was just getting started as a psychic when he came to me for a reading—he gave me that old Tarot deck and a hand-written notebook on the Qabalah, which I had for many years and which is the basis of *Qabalah, Tarot & the Western Mystery Tradition*. I saw him only two or three times and, oddly enough, I never learned his name."

The Tarot Atu is a version of the Marseilles Tarot, and only slightly different from the one now in general circulation. Although the author refers to the Tarot Atu in the text, the student of these rituals should know that the Marseilles Tarot would be the appropriate deck to use.

The Publisher

DEDICATED

To All True Seekers of the Light

May what they find herein
sustain them in their search
for the Quintessence,
the Stone of the Wise,
the Summum Bonum,
True Wisdom and
Perfect Happiness.

A Note to the Reader

Dear Seeker:

A path is opening before you, a path that will allow you to break out of your present circle of limited awareness. This is the path of New Age Qabalah. The term "New Age" indicates the forward-looking attitude of Aquarius—whose keynote is "Freedom." We seek freedom to be, freedom to become.

This book is *not* a study of the Hebrew Qabalah. It is a study of the *Hermetic-Gnostic* Qabalah. Both systems share the primary symbol of the Qabalah, the Tree of Life. This is the basis of our study. This book is also not just another tired re-hash of what was so brilliantly done by the late nineteenth-century Hermetic Order of the Golden Dawn. It's a fresh approach.

All honor and respect to the Jewish Rabbis of olden times, steeped in Hebraic mysticism. All honor and respect to the students, practitioners and teachers of Hermeticism, Gnosticism, Esotericism, Astrology, Alchemy, Illuminism, Ceremonial Magic, Neo-Platonism, who from pre-Christian times to the present have given us what we speak of as the Western Mystery Tradition. In our study we shall eagerly harken to their voices and drink deeply from the cups they offer.

What most people see, touch and feel is only a minuscule part of a greater reality. This everyday world of "normal" sense perception is infinitesimally small compared to an infinitely greater cosmos that is perceivable to "para-normal" sensory apparatus, which all of us possess but which most of us know little or nothing about. "Enlightenment" is emergence from the darkness of our previously limited sense perceptions into a knowledge of and participation in that greater reality. That's what this study is all about.

To work well together we need to know each other. I was born at 5:30 A.M. on Saturday, March 19, 1910, in Huntington, West Virginia. I was the youngest son of Riley Monroe Bias and Mary Elizabeth Jenkins Bias. Before I was six years old I made a "playlike" Elizabethan theatre of sticks and stones in our back yard. I knew that the stage should be a raised platform, that the "town dandies" sat on either side of the stage to witness the performance, that a "window" at the back of the stage was where "the Gods" and "ghosts" appeared. I was a boy actor in the time of William Shakespeare, but I still don't know if I ever knew him. Along with this experience of partially remembering a former incarnation, I developed psychokinesis. My sister was "keeping company," and she, her beau and several neighborhood friends became interested in "making the table walk." Several people would put their palms-down hands on a small table, sing a song, and ask, "Is there a spirit present who could answer our questions?" There were slight jerks and small tentative movements of the table until I went into the room with cookies and lemonade my mother had fixed for my sister and her guests. The table seemingly became "alive," tilting on two legs, literally dancing about the room. After I was dragged from under the couch, covered with spilled lemonade and crumbled cookies, they had me put my hands on the table. I can still remember the "feel" of that little round three-legged table; it quivered and vibrated under my hands and would readily, almost eagerly, tilt when asked a question. Of course, the questions asked by that group of young people were such deep philosophical ones as, "Does my boy friend really love me?", "How many children will I have?" and "Will I be married more than once?" This went on for several once-or-twice a week sessions until one night, while the table was tilting merrily away, a large gilt-framed picture lifted itself from its supporting nail and crashed to the floor. Hearing the noise of the crash, my mother came rushing into the room, surveyed the scene, and firmly announced, "No more of this!" That put an end to my career as a boy medium.

All my life has been spent with the psychic and the occult. My inherent psychic abilities naturally developed of their own accord. From the time I was first allowed into the adult section of the Huntington Public Library, I read voraciously every book I could find on the subjects of Occultism, Transcendentalism, Mysticism, Spiritualism, Psychic Phenomena, New Thought, and kindred subjects. I organized and conducted a Spiritualist Church in Huntington, was ordained in 1937 into the ministry by Rev. Amanda Coffman Flower, president of the Independent Spiritualist Association, and have served as a minister of churches in Jackson, Michigan; Buffalo, New York; Toledo, Ohio; St. Petersburg, Florida, and New York, N.Y. where I currently live. I helped organize the Spiritualist-Episcopal Church and the Universal Spiritualist Association. I have served as staff psychic, educational director, and president of the Indiana Association of Spiritualists which owns and operates Camp Chesterfield in Chesterfield, Indiana. I have served churches as a guest speaker, psychic, teacher in twelve states. I am at present dean of the Universal Spiritualist Institute which holds sessions each summer on various Mid-Western college campuses. I have been honored, praised, castigated, jailed, in connection with my work in the psychic field. I've been around.

Other than the rearrangement of the material, there is very little that is totally new in this study. Besides the "mouth to ear" communication of esoteric teaching from my spiritual mentor, Father Amos, I have received much from the writings of Alice Bailey, Franz Bardon, Helena Petrovna Blavatsky, Joseph Campbell, Paul Foster Case, Aleister Crowley, Homer Curtiss, Mircea Eliade, Dion Fortune, William G. Gray, G.I. Gurdjieff, Franz Hartmann, Max Heindel, Carl G. Jung, H.B. Leadbeater, Alan Leo, Eliphas Levi, S.L. MacGregor Mathers, G.R.S. Mead, Stainton Moses, F.W.H. Myers, P.D. Ouspensky, A.E. Powell, Israel Regardie, Rudolf Steiner, Arthur Edward Waite, W.W. Westcott, Colin Wilson and many others, to whom I am deeply indebted and eternally grateful.

I give you the traditional witches' greeting: Blessed be!

Clifford Bias

How to Use This Book

1. Do you have a good dictionary? If not, buy, beg, borrow, but don't steal one. And start using it.

2. Who are you? Why are you where you are and as you are at this particular time? Might there be a purpose for your life? To begin to find some answers, or even to find that there are no specific answers at this specific time, please begin a "Magical Journal." Write a brief biographical sketch of yourself, like mine in the Preface: Name, time and place of birth, parents' names, any interesting incidents in early life.

3. Please read and consider the "Inducement" on page xxiii. Do you think this is a somewhat drastic, perhaps even cruel, way for a man to help his kid brother to learn to swim? Think of the man as an excellent swimmer who loves his little brother. He is right there and ready to jump in with assistance if any is needed. Please memorize and never forget: "It is ever the duty of the brother or sister above to stoop to help the brother or sister below." If I want help from those above I must give help to those below. This is a law. And the type and manner and amount of help is the decision of the giver, *not* the asker.

4. Please read aloud the Prelude on page xix. Two, perhaps unfamiliar but fundamental, occult concepts face us here. First is the idea of cosmic periodicity—that *before* this universe of ours came into existence there were *other* ones that preceded it. Or, to put it a little differently, the cosmos has periods of existence or manifestation

Table 1. *The Hebrew Alphabet*

Letter	Name	Latin	Phonetic	Numerical Value		Word Value	Equivalent
אָ	אָלֶף	Aleph	Ah'Leff	1	M	Ox or Bull	A
בּ	בֵּת	Beth	Bayth	2	D	House	Bh, V, B
גּ	גִּמֶל	Gimel	Gemel	3	D	Camel	Gh, G
דּ	דָּלֶת	Daleth	Dahl'eth	4	D	Door	Dh, D
ה	הֵ	He	Hay	5		Window	H
ו	וָ	Vau	Wow	6		Nail	W
ז	זַיִן	Zain	Zah'yeen	7		Sword	Z
ח	חֵת	Cheth	K'ath	8		Field	Ch
ט	טֵת	Teth	Tath	9		Serpent	T
י	יֹד	Yod	Yodh	10		Hand	Y
כ	כַּף	Kaph	Kaff	20	D	Closed Hand	Kh, K
ל	לָמֶד	Lamed	Lahm'ed	30		Oxgoad	L
מ	מֵם	Mem	Mam	40	M	Water	M
נ	נוּן	Nun	Noon	50		Fish	N
ס	סָמֶח	Samech	Saum'ekh	60		A Prop	S
ע	עַיִן	Ayin	Ah'yeen	70		Eye	O
פ	פֵה	Pe	Pay	80	D	Mouth	Ph, F, P
צ	צָדֵי	Tzaddi	Tzahddi	90		Fish Hook	Ts, X
ק	קוּף	Qoph	Quof	100		Back of Head	Q
ר	רֵאש	Resh	Rash	200	D	Head or Face	R
ש	שִׁן	Shin	Sheen	300	M	Teeth	Sh, Sch, S
ת	תָו	Tau	Tah'oo	400	D	Cross	Th, T

FINAL LETTERS					
ך Kaph 500	ם Mem 600	ן Nun 700	ף Pe 800	ץ Tzaddi 900	א 1000

alternating with periods of non-existence or un-manifestation. The Hindus speak of this as "The Days and Nights of Brahm." A "day" cycle of manifestation they call a "Manvantara"; the "night" period of world-rest is called "Pralaya." The same idea is the Qabalistic use of *Ruach Elohim* (Roo-ach El-oh-heem), the Breath of God, inhalation and exhalation; God's inbreathing and outbreathing being the great cycle of life out of and into manifestation. Stop and think about this for a moment.

The other occult concept that is perhaps unfamiliar to many of us is the idea of "Negative Existence" with its "Three Veils." These words refer to those aspects of God, or that nature of God, or those dimensions of God, which is or are completely beyond human comprehension. For convenience sake we may call this the Absolute—and we must content ourselves for now with the saying that the Absolute is unknown to the state of consciousness that is normal to human beings. And let us realize that when we mention the "Veils," they correspond to human limitations, not to cosmic conditions. Stop and think about this for a while.

5. Let's turn now to the Hebrew Alphabet, shown in Table 1. I repeat that this course is *not* a study of the Hebrew Qabalah. But we do use certain Hebrew elements in the Hermetic-Gnostic Qabalah, notably the famous glyph, the Tree of Life. *And* the Hebrew Alphabet. Which we have to learn. So, let's start. Look closely at each letter. Check the third and fourth columns where you'll find the Latin and the Phonetic pronunciation. Say aloud each letter many, many times while you examine it closely.

Hebrew is written from *right* to *left.* The word Qabalah is spelled in Hebrew *Quof, Beth, Lamed,* the English equivalents of which are Q B L. If we were to write it in Hebrew, it would go like this:

L	B	Q
Lamed	Beth	Quof

The word is pronounced Kuh-BALL-uh. It means "to receive" with the implication of "received teaching."

6. Read *Sepher Yetzirah,* The Book of Formation, on page 3, two or three times silently, getting the gist, the meaning. Then read it aloud, slowly and reverently.

7. Please read several times *The Lightning Flash* on page 15. Study, study, study, practically memorize to the point that you can answer without hesitation and without referring to the text such questions as: What are the gems of Binah? What planet is associated with Chokmah? What is Arikh Anpin? Name the Ten Emanations of Divinity. What does each name mean? What is the Abyss? What are the Three Magic Images of Tiphareth? What planet is associated with Netzach? With Hod? What similarity is there between Binah and Malkuth?

8. Read the *Path of the Serpent*, in Part II. Again, study the correspondences until you know them by heart. Study Figure 6 on page 36, and Figure 7 on 37. Internalize the elements in the Formula of the Tetragrammaton. Study the diagram of the universal self and the greater universe. What do the symbols stand for? What is the relationship of your self to the greater universe?

9. Study, study, study! When you have thoroughly digested the material in Parts I and II, then you are ready for the *real* work to begin: the *Rituals of Return*, Part III of this book. This is work you will do on your own. The Rituals of Return are presented in the order that they must be performed.

Prelude

BEFORE THE BEGINNING

Hear, O Seeker:
Before the beginning, no thing existed.

But there is no beginning and there is no end, there is only change. The wise know this, saying there is day and night in the universe; declaring the cosmic day to be a thousand ages in span and the night a thousand ages. Thus when we speak of a "beginning" we mean the start of this present cosmic day. So let us repeat:

Before the beginning, no thing existed.
That no thing is God unmanifest,
God unmanifest is Negative Existence.

Negative Existence is of three degrees or natures, One in Three and Three in One, all-containing yet uncontained. It is the thrice unknown. The three degrees or natures are called Veils.

0.
The first Veil, which shall be the last, is *Ain*, which is No,
Negativity, Zero Absolute, Undefinable.

0.0
The second Veil is *Ain Soph*, No Thing, also Undefinable.

0.0.0
The third Veil is *Ain Soph Aur*, the Limitless Light, the
Radiant Darkness.

Ain Soph Aur, the Limitless Light, the Radiant Darkness, is the Zero
as basis of possible vibration. It is described as the Circle whose
center is everywhere and whose circumference is nowhere. Its center
is everywhere. Its circumference is nowhere. Everywhere. Nowhere.

Ain Soph Aur is the Ancient of all the Ancients. It is the Egg of the
Cosmos, The Cosmic Egg. It is pictured as the *Uroboros*, the serpent
biting its tail. It is beyond all comprehension.

Ain Soph Aur, the Limitless Light, the Radiant Darkness, is Supreme
Silence. It is Absolute Rest. It is the Absolute at rest. Naught but
Silence can express its true name and nature.

It is the Egyptian *Amoun*, the Concealed, the God who cannot be
known. It is *Nu*, the state of inactivity. It is *Parabrahm*. It is the *Tao*.

There is a reality even prior to heaven and earth;
Indeed, it has no form, much less a name;
Eyes fail to see it;
It has no voice for ears to detect;
To call it Mind or Buddha violates its nature,
For it then becomes like a visionary flower in the air;
It is not Mind, nor Buddha;
Absolutely quiet, and yet illuminating in a mysterious way,
It allows itself to be perceived only by the clear-eyed.
It is Dharma truly beyond form and sound;
It is Tao having nothing to do with words.

It is God at rest. The Cosmic Breath is indrawn and held.

BEING

Ain Soph Aur has no center since it is everywhere and nowhere. But by its very nature it concentrates a center. It focuses a point. It erupts a beginning.

God stirs. Day dawns.

Instantly a flash of lightning issues from but is contained within Negative Existence. This Lightning Flash forms Ten Emanations of Deity called the *Sephiroth* (suh-FIE-roth). Each one is a *Sephira* (suh-FEAR-uh). Remember, O Seeker, ten and not nine, ten and not eleven, ten are the Sephiroth.

The ten holy Sephiroth are: *Kether* (KETHur), the Crown; *Chokmah* (HOKE-muh), Wisdom; *Binah* (BEE-nuh), Understanding; *Chesed* (HAY-sed), Mercy; *Geburah* (guh-BOOR-uh and/or juh-BOO-ruh), Strength; *Tiphareth* (TIFF-uh-reth), Beauty; *Netzach* (NET-zahk), Victory; *Hod* (rhymes with *lode* and *road*), Splendor; *Yesod* (YAY-sode), Foundation; and *Malkuth* (MAHL-kooth), the Kingdom.

Centerless Ain Soph Aur concentrating a center, focusing a point, erupting a beginning, is God stirring, or as some say, God awakening. In the beginning, God. God *is* the beginning.

> God is God.
> Shema Yisroel Adonai Elohenu, Adonai Echod.
> (shuh-MAH YISS-ro-el AH-doh-NOH-ee EL-oh-hay-noo,
>   AH-doh-NOH-ee A-hahd).
> Hear, O Israel, the Lord is God, the Lord is One.
> One is god: Omnipotent, Omniscient, Omnipresent.
> God is the Absolute, The Absolute is God.
> This is *Eheieh* (ee-HEE-yuh), Existence of Existences, Pure
>   Existence.
> Breathe out, breathe in, breathe out. Thus you pronounce
>   the God-Name Eheieh.

Eheieh is usually translated I Am That I Am. But its more current translation is I Am Who I Am.

I am not lonesome nor apart that men should cry, "Lo, there!"
I am the all, immersed in all, behold me everywhere;
I am the morning zephyr soft while skipping o'er the lea,
I am the music of the brook that flows on to the sea;
I am the kisses of the sun, I am the tears of the rain,
I am the welcome breath of spring that brings new life again;
I am the sprouting of the seed, the budding of the flower,
I am the beauty that men behold unfolding every hour;
I am the singing of the birds, the rustling of the leaves,
I am the holy force of life in everything that breathes;
I am the thrill of harmony men feel but cannot tell,
I am the firm unchanging law that worketh all things well;
I am the source that all men seek, I am their peace, their pain,
I am the courage of the weak that turns all loss to gain;
I am the hope that never dies, the ecstasy divine,
I am the Great Eternal Love that draws all life to mine;
I am the light that never fails, the power that never dies,
I am the still, small voice within that bids the Soul arise;
I am the fruit of highest thought, I am the iron rod
That strengthens and supports the whole, I AM what men call GOD.

Inducement

"Teach me to swim," the younger asked the older brother.

The man picked up the boy and threw him into deep water.

"Swim," he said.

Part I

The Way Down

Sepher Yetzirah
(The Book of Formation)

THE TEXT IN FIFTEEN PARAGRAPHS

1. In thirty-two wonderful Paths of Wisdom did Yah, the Lord of Hosts, the Living God, King of the Universe, the merciful and gracious God, the Exalted One, the Dweller in Eternity, most high and holy, engrave His Name by three Sepharim: Numbers, Letters and Sounds, which in Him are one and the same thing.

2. Ten are the ineffable Sephiroth, Twenty-Two are the Letters, the foundation of all things, they are Three Mothers, Seven Double and Twelve Simple Letters.

3. Ten is the number of the ineffable Sephiroth, ten and not nine, ten and not eleven. Understand this wisdom and be wise in its perception. Search out concerning it, restore the Word to its creator and replace Him who formed it upon His throne.

4. The ten ineffable Sephiroth have ten vast regions associated with them; boundless in origin and having no ending; an abyss of good and of ill; measureless height and depth, an abyss of the East and an abyss of the West, an abyss of the North and an abyss of the South; and the Lord, the Faithful King, rules all these from His holy seat in the midst of them, forever and ever.

5. The ten ineffable Sephiroth have the appearance of the Lightning Flash, their origin is unseen and no end is perceived. The Word is in them as they rush forth, and as they return they speak as from the whirlwind, and returning, fall prostrate in adoration before the Throne.

6. The ten ineffable Sephiroth, whose ending is even as their origin, are like as a flame arising from a burning coal. For God is superlative in His unity, there is none equal unto Him. What number canst thou place before One?

7. From No-Thing He made Some-Thing, from the empty Void He made all the worlds, from the non-existent He brought forth everything that has been produced and everything that hath Life; and the production of all things by means of the twenty-two letters is the proof that they are all but parts of one whole.

8. The twenty-two sounds and letters are the foundation of all things, three Mothers, seven Doubles and twelve Simples.

9. The three Mothers are Aleph, Mem and Shin. They are Air, Water and Fire. Water is silent, Fire is sibilant, and Air derived from Spirit is as the tongue of a balance standing between the contraries which are in equilibrium, reconciling and mediating between them.

10. The three Mothers in the World are Aleph, Mem and Shin; the heavens were produced from Fire, the earth from Water, and the Air from Spirit is as a reconciler between the Fire and the Water.

11. The three Mothers, Aleph, Mem and Shin, Fire, Water and Air, are shown in the year; from the Fire was made heat and from the Water was made cold and from Air was produced the temperate state as a mediator between them. The three Mothers, Aleph, Mem and Shin, Fire, Water and Air, are found in man; from the Fire was formed the head, from the Water the belly, and from the Air was formed the chest, again a mediator between the others.

12. The seven Double Letters are Beth, Gimel, Daleth, Kaph, Pe, Resh and Tau. They are referred to Life, Peace, Wisdom, Riches, Grace, Fertility and Power. They each have two sounds, the hard and the soft, the aspirated and the softened. They are called Double because each Letter presents a contrast or permutation: Life and Death, Peace and War, Wisdom and Folly, Riches and Poverty, Grace and Disgrace, Fertility and Solitude, Power and Servitude.

13. The seven Double Letters He designed, produced and combined to form the Seven Sacred Planets of the Solar System, Sun, Moon, Mars, Mercury, Jupiter, Venus and Saturn; the Seven Days of the Week; the Seven Gates of the Soul which are the two eyes, the two ears, the mouth and the two nostrils. The seven Double Letters are also the Seven Days of Creation, the Seven Heavens, the Seven Earths and the Seven Sabbaths. For this cause He has loved and blessed the number Seven more than all things under Heaven, His Throne.

14. The twelve Simple Letters are He, Vau, Zain, Cheth, Teth, Yod, Lamed, Nun, Samech, Ain, Tzaddi and Qoph. They are the foundations of these twelve properties: Sight, Hearing, Smell, Taste, Touch, Sexual Love, Work, Movement, Anger, Mirth, Imagination and Sleep. He designed and combined the twelve Simple Letters and formed with them the twelve Signs of the Zodiac, Aries, Taurus, Gemini, Cancer, Leo, Virgo, Libra, Scorpio, Sagittarius, Capricorn, Aquarius and Pisces. The twelve are the Months of the Year, Nisan, Yiar, Sivan, Tamuz, Ab, Elul, Tishri, Hesvan, Kislev, Tebet, Sabat and Adar. They are also the twelve organs, the brain, the heart, the two lungs, the two kidneys, the spleen, the liver, the gall, the sexual apparatus, stomach and intestines. He made these and arranged them in order of battle for welfare.

15. Behold now these are the Twenty and Two Letters, Three Mothers, Seven Doubles and Twelve Simples, from which Yah, Jehovah, Tzabaoth, the Elohim of the living, the Dweller in Eternity formed and established all things, High and Holy is His Name.

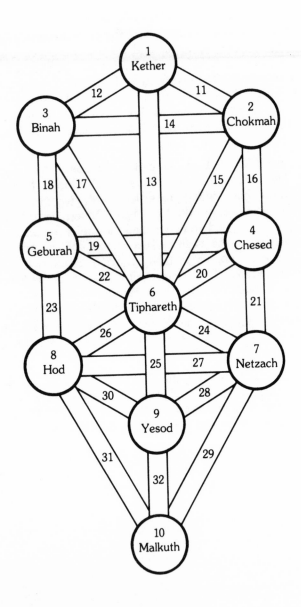

Figure 1. The Paths of Wisdom on the Tree of Life.

The Thirty-Two Paths of Wisdom

1 *Kether* — The Crown

The First Path is called the Admirable Intelligence, the Highest Crown, for it is the Light giving the power of comprehension of the First Principle which has no beginning and no end, and it is the Primal Glory for no created being can attain to its essence.

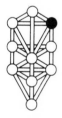

2 *Chokmah* — Wisdom

The Second Path is that of the Illuminating Intelligence, it is the reflection of the Crown of Creation, the Splendor of the Unity, equalling it, and is named the Second Glory.

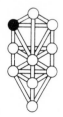

3 *Binah* — Understanding

The Third Path is the Wonderful Intelligence and it is the Mother of Faith for from Her doth faith emanate.

3-4 *Daath* — Knowledge

The Unnumbered Path is the Sanctifying Intelligence for by the Union of Wisdom and Understanding are things sanctified and made holy.

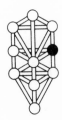

4 *Chesed* — Mercy

The Fourth Path is named Measuring, Cohesive or Receptacular and it is so called because it contains holy powers and from it emanates spiritual virtues.

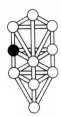

5 *Geburah* — Strength

The Fifth Path is called the Radical Intelligence because it is the Channel of the Holy One's Might, Protection, Retribution and Vengeance.

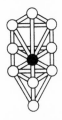

6 *Tiphareth* — Beauty

The Sixth Path is called the Intelligence of the Mediating Influence because in it are manifested and multiplied the influxes that flow from and into all the reservoirs of the Blessings.

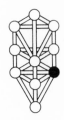

7 *Netzach* — Victory

The Seventh Path is the Occult or Hidden Intelligence because its love underlies and illumines as from within the activities of all the lights.

8 *Hod* — Splendor

The Eighth Path is called the Resplendent Intelligence because it is the Refulgent Splendor of all the Intellectual Virtues which are perceived by the eyes of intellect.

9 *Yesod* — Foundation

The Ninth Path is the Intelligence of Separative Influence because by it the emanations are separated and reformed and empowered to operate the Machinery of the Universe.

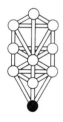

10 *Malkuth* — The Kingdom

The Tenth Path is the Corporeal Intelligence and is so called because it is the body which is formed beneath the whole order of the worlds and is the increment of them.

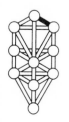

11 (connects *Kether* and *Chokmah*)

Aleph . . . . AIR . . . . Ox

The Eleventh Path is the Scintillating Intelligence because it is the essence of the curtain which is played close to the order of the disposition, and this is a special dignity given to it that it may be able to stand before the Face of the Cause of Causes.

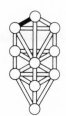

12   (connects *Kether* and *Binah*)

Mem . . . . WATER . . . . Water

The Twelfth Path is the Intelligence of Transparency because it is that species of Magnificence called Seership and which is named the place whence issues the vision of those seeing apparitions and whence issue the prophecies made by seers.

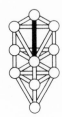

13   (connects *Kether* and *Tiphareth*)

Shin . . . . FIRE . . . . Tooth or Fang

The Thirteenth Path is the Illuminating Intelligence and is so called because it is that Chanel of Scintillating Flame which is the founder of the concealed and fundamental ideas of holiness and of their stages of preparation.*

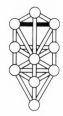

14   (connects *Chokmah* and *Binah*)

Cheth . . . . . SATURN . . . . . Fence or Field

The Fourteenth Path is named the Uniting Intelligence and is so called because it is itself the Essence of Glory in the Consummation of Love.

15   (connects *Chokmah* and *Tiphareth*)

Zayin . . . . LEO . . . . Sword

The Fifteenth Path is the Luminous Intelligence because it is the Shining Way transmitting Power from Father to Child.

---

*Editor's note: The Sepher Yetzirah specifically assigns the Simple Letters to the Signs of the Zodiac but in these rituals the Simple Letter Cheth is assigned to the planet Saturn and Path 14. The reason for this is the greater appropriateness of the symbolism of the correspondences.

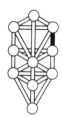

16   (connects *Chokmah* and *Chesed*)
Vau . . . . TAURUS . . . . Nail

The Sixteenth Path is the Triumphal Intelligence because it is the Glory of Established Strength and is also called Paradise for the Righteous.

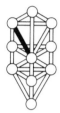

17   (connects *Binah* and *Tiphareth*)
Tzaddi . . . . CANCER . . . . Fish Hook

The Seventeenth Path is the Disposing Intelligence which provides Faith to the Righteous and disposes them to Service, the foundation of excellence in higher things.

18   (connects *Binah* and *Geburah*)
Teth . . . . SCORPIO . . . . Serpent

The Eighteenth Path is the Intelligence of Probation and is so called because it is the Primary Temptation.

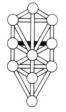

19   (connects *Chesed* and *Geburah*)
Heh . . . . LIBRA . . . . Window

The Nineteenth Path is the Intelligence of the Secret of Spiritual Activities and is so called because it is the Essence of Equilibrium.

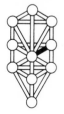

20   (connects *Chesed* and *Tiphareth*)
Resh . . . . . . JUPITER . . . . . . Head or Face

The Twentieth Path is the Intelligence of Conciliation because it receives and transmits the divine influence of the benediction upon all and each existence.

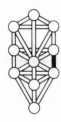

21 (connects *Chesed* and *Netzach*)

Yod . . . . VIRGO . . . . Hand

The Twenty-First Path is the Stable Intelligence that has the Virtue of Consistency among all Numerations and is idealistically Discriminative.

22 (connects *Geburah* and *Tiphareth*)

Kaph . . . . MARS . . . . Fist

The Twenty-Second Path is the Faithful Intelligence because its spiritual virtues are increased and all dwellers of earth are under its shadow.

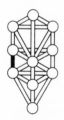

23 (connects *Geburah* and *Hod*)

Ayin . . . . GEMINI . . . . Eye

The Twenty-Third Path is the Intelligence of the House of Influence by the greatness of whose abundance the influx of good things is increased.

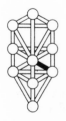

24 (connects *Tiphareth* and *Netzach*)

Daleth . . . . VENUS . . . . Door

The Twenty-Fourth Path is the Imaginative Intelligence and it is so called because it gives a lovely likeness to all the similitudes which are created in a manner similar to its harmonious elegancies.

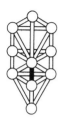

25 (connects *Tiphareth* and *Yesod*)

Beth . . . . SUN . . . . House

The Twenty-Fifth Path is called the Administrative Intelligence since it directs all the operations of the planets and concurs therein.

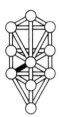

26 (connects *Tiphareth* and *Hod*)

Peh . . . . MERCURY . . . . Mouth

The Twenty-Sixth Path is the Serving Intelligence acting as Messenger and Intellectual Companion of Tiphareth and leads souls from Darkness into Light.

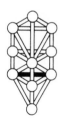

27 (connects *Netzach* and *Hod*)

Samech . . . . SAGITTARIUS . . . . Prop

The Twenty-Seventh Path is called the Renovating Intelligence because the Holy God renews by it all the changing things both great and small.

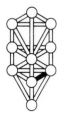

28 (connects *Netzach* and *Yesod*)

Lamed . . . . ARIES . . . . Ox Goad

The Twenty-Eighth Path is the Intelligence of Will because by it is perfected the nature of all things under the Orb of the Sun.

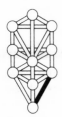

29   (connects *Netzach* and *Malkuth*)
Nun . . . . PISCES . . . . Fish

The Twenty-Ninth Path is the Constituting Intelligence because it makes up the substance of creation in pure darkness, that darkness spoken of in Job 38:9 "and thick darkness a swaddling band for it."

30   (connects *Hod* and *Yesod*)
Qoph . . . . . CAPRICORN. . . . . Back of Head

The Thirtieth Path is the Exciting Intelligence because thence is ruled instincts of men and animals and it acts as Regent until the Prince takes the throne.*

31   (connects *Hod* and *Malkuth*)
Gimel . . . . AQUARIUS . . . . Camel

The Thirty-First Path is the Collecting Intelligence and it is so called because Astrologers deduce from it the judgments of the Celestial Signs and Planets.

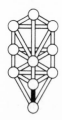

32   (connects *Yesod* and *Malkuth*)
Tau . . . . MOON. . . . . Cross

The Thirty-Second Path is the Perpetual Intelligence because it rules the movements of the Moon and perfects all the revolutions of the Zodiac.

---

*The Sepher Yetzirah specifically assigns the Double Letters to the planets, but here the double letter Gimel is assigned to the sign of Aquarius and Path 31 of the Tree. The reason for this is the greater appropriateness of the symbolism of the correspondences.

The Ten Holy Sephiroth
on The Qabalistic Sword
(The Lightning Flash)

THE SUPERNALS

Kether, Chokmah and Binah together are called the Three Supernals, the Supernal Triad.

1 *Kether* — The Crown

The Admirable Intelligence. Kether is the Supreme Unity, the ONE before whom NOTHING EXISTS, the ONE who is the ALL and the ALL who is the ONE. The God-Name is *Eheieh*, I Am That I Am. This is *Aum, Amoun, Amen, Brahma, Khepera, Neb-er-tcher,* Lord of the Universe. It is *Arikanpin, Macroprosopus* the Vast Countenance, the White Head, the Ancient of ALL the Ancients. The Magic Image is an ancient bearded King seen in right profile. Kether is the Rashith ha Galagahim, the Sphere of the Primum Mobile, the first whirling motions, symbolized by the Fylfot Cross, the Swastika. Other symbols are the Point within the Circle, the Lamp over the Altar, the Soaring Hawk, the Almond in Flower and a flawless Diamond. On the Queen Scale of Colors Kether is Pure White Brilliance. The perfume is Ambergris. Kether is the Root and Principle of Air—the Ruach, the Breath, Prana, Pneuma, Spiritus—the Life Principle itself, the vital principle of all that is. Microcosmically it is the Monad, the Atman, the Yeckidah.

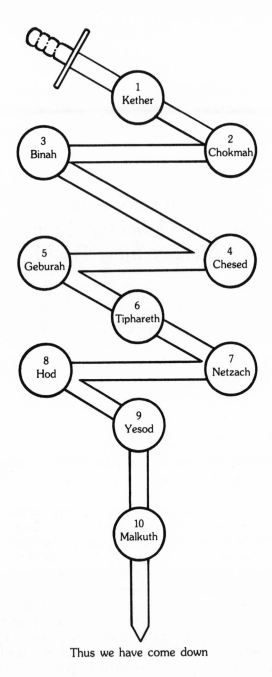

Thus we have come down

Figure 2. The Qabalistic Sword, also called The Path of the Lightning Flash.

2   Chokmah — Wisdom

The Illuminating Intelligence. Chokmah is God the Male, God the Father-Son containing the Chiah, the Creative Energy. The God-Name is *Yah-weh* or Jehovah, Essence of Being. This is the Supernal Father, *Ab, Abba, Yah*. It is the Yod of Tetragrammaton. Chokmah is space. This the Sphere of the Zodiac, the Sphere of the Fixed Stars, Mazloth the Sky, Nut or Nuit the Sky, Uranus as the Starry Heaven, thus also the Sphere of Uranus. Chokmah is the root and principle of fire. This is the Generative Power symbolized by the Uplifted Rod or Wand of Power, the Straight Line, the Red Upward Pointing Equilateral Triangle, the Tower, the Spire, the Steeple, the Lingam, the Phallus, and is called the Inner Robe of Glory. The Magic Image is a Bearded Male Figure or any Father Image. The gems are the Turquoise and the Star Ruby. The plant is the Amaranth. The Eagle, the Hawk, the Swan are sacred to Chokmah. The Queen Scale color of Chokmah is that of semen, Grey. The perfume is musk. The metal is Uranium and all radioactive substances. Chokmah is the yang, positive, masculine, dry, hot. It is the Eternal Masculine, the mysterious Father-Brother-Husband-Son male. The Chiah, the Animus.

3   Binah — Understanding

The Wonderful Intelligence, God the Female, God the Mother. The God-Name is *Elohim*, a word whose root, El, is masculine singular but whose ending is feminine plural, thus meaning God with the implication of Gods or Goddess. Binah is the Great Mother, the Door of Life with two aspects: *Aima* the bright fertile mother, and *Ama* the dark sterile mother. Binah is the *Anima Mundi*, the Soul of the World, the Supernal Mother, the first He of Tetragrammaton. She is *Marah*, the Great Sea. She is MARY the Queen of Heaven. She is the Lady of Ten Thousand Appellations—many-named is she: Isis, Sakti, Tefnut, Cybele, Demeter, Rhea, Hera, Juno, Frigga, Kwan-yin and many another. Binah is the root and principle of water. In the waters of the Great Sea Life took its first forms. Binah is the Sacred Womb holding and preserving Life. Her symbols include the Cup, the Chalice, the Well, the Cave, the Blue Downward Pointing Equilateral Triangle, the Yoni—called the Outer Robe of Concealment. Her Queen Scale color is Black, The Magic Image is a Matron. Binah is the

Sphere of Neptune. Her perfume is Myrrh. Her gems are the Pearl and the Star Sapphire. The Lily and the Lotus are hers, as are the Peacock, the Bee, the Sow, the Cow and the Lioness. In Chemistry she is Oxygen. She is the Yin, negative, feminine, damp, cold. She is the Eternal Feminine, the mysterious Mother-Sister-Wife-Daughter female. The Anima, the Neshamah.

DAATH

Chokmah is Force. Binah is Form. Their conjunction is, becomes or produces a Sephira which is hidden; a Sephira which has no number; a Sephira which is not shown on the path of the Lightning Flash. Its name is Daath.

Daath — Knowledge

The Sanctifying Intelligence. This is the Male-Female conjoined in Sexual Embrace. The God-Name is Tetragrammaton-Elohim or Yahweh-Elohim, God of Gods. Daath is the Sphere of Saturn, Shabbathai. Daath is Knowledge. "To Know" is here in the Biblical sense, as when a man "knows" his wife. Daath is the first hidden union of Chokmah and Binah, of Yang and Yin, of Wisdom and Understanding. Daath is also the first and hidden product of that union. Daath is hidden by the Abyss. Daath is the "Fall of the Angels."

THE ABYSS

Separating the Three Supernals and the seven lower Sephiroth is a vast chasm called the Abyss. The force of the Lightning Flash is braked or slowed down in crossing the Abyss. It also changes polarity in the crossing.

4 Chesed — Mercy

Gedullah, Magnificence. The Measuring, Cohesive, Receptacular Intelligence. God-Name: El, God the Creator. This is Amoun, Brahma, Zeus, Jupiter, Jove, Wotan in the capacity of the Loving, Kind, Righteous, Magnanimous, Majestic and Merciful All-Father. He is VISHNU, the Preserver of Beings. Chesed is *Tzedeg*, the Sphere of Jupiter. It represents the Anabolic, the upbuilding Aspect of Force. This is the Lord as the Good Shepherd. "The Lord is my shepherd, I shall not want." His representative is the Pope, Il Papa, the Bishop, the Priest as Father, the Minister or Rabbi as Pastor. Chesed, Mercy, is Beneficence, Benevolence, the religion of the Fatherhood of God, depicting God as the Loving Father, kind and merciful. The Magic Image is a Mighty Crowned and Throned King. His instruments are the Shepherd's Crook, the King's Sceptre. On the Queen's Scale Chesed's color is Blue. His odor is Cedar. His gems are the Lapis Lazuli, the Amethyst and the Sapphire. The Olive, Cedar and Shamrock are sacred to him. The fabled Unicorn is his pet. Chesed is the Will to Exist, the Life Wish.

5 Geburah — Strength

Pachad, Fear. The Radical Intelligence. The God-Name is Elohim Gebor, God the Potent. Geburah represents the Catabolic, Down-Breaking, Aspect of Force. Another name for it is Severity. It is Cruelty. It is Destruction. The Magic Image is a Mighty Warrior in his Chariot. This is Horus as Lord of Force, Nephthys as the Lady of Severity. It is Siva, the Destroyer of Beings, Kali the Destroyer, Ares, Lord of War, Mars the War God, Thor. Geburah is *Madim*, the Sphere of Mars, the Lord of Battles, The God of Vengeance. The weapons of Geburah are the Sword, the Spear, the Scourge, the Chain. The Queen Scale color is Scarlet. Geburah's odors are hot metal, gunsmoke and burning sulfur. The minerals are Iron, Steel, Sulfur. His tree is the Hickory. His animal is the fabled Basilisk which slays with its glance. His gem is the Ruby. Geburah is the Will to Not Exist, the Death Wish.

6 Tiphareth — Beauty

The Intelligence of Mediating Influence. Chokmah is God the Father, Binah is God the Mother, Tiphareth is God the Son. It is the Vau of

Tetragrammaton, the Holy Logos, the Word of God. From the point of view of Kether, Tiphareth is a child. This is the Christ Child, Ben the Son, Horus the Child, Hoor-par-Krat or Harpocrates the Child, Aurora as Goddess of the Dawn. The Magic Image is a child, usually male. From the point of view of Malkuth, Tiphareth is a King. This is Melekh the King, Asar or Osiris, Rama, Krishna, Lord Buddha, Christ the King. The Magic Image is a Majestic King. From the point of view of the transformation of force (it is in Tiphareth that descending force is transmuted into form) Tiphareth is the sacrificed god. This is Christ suffering his Passion, Adonis, Dionysus, Bacchus. The Magic Image is the Crucifixion. Tiphareth is *Shemesh,* the Sphere of Sol, the Sun This is Ra, Amoun or Amon Ra, Apollo. It is the planetary Christ, the solar logos. Ever is Tiphareth the avatar, the Incarnation of God in human form. This is Osiris, Rama, Krishna, Gautama the Buddha, Jesus the Christ, Mithras. Tiphareth is the Mediator between God and man. It is the Ego between the self and the personality. This is the Manas, the Aib. But first and foremost is Tiphareth the Savior God. And remember that Tiphareth is also the Spirit Self of man, the real man, the Self, the Christ-Within-Self, the Buddhic Self, Man the Son, the Son of Man. The God-Name of Tiphareth is Tetragrammaton *Aloah Va Daath*, God the Strong. The symbols are the Calvary Cross, the Rosy Cross, the Eucharistic Host and Wine, the Lamen, The Dagger. The color is Golden Yellow. The perfume is Olibanum, an aromatic gum resin of trees of the genus Boswellia. The mineral is Gold. The animals are the Phoenix, the Lion, the Pelican (feeding its young with its own blood.) The gems are the Topaz and the yellow Diamond. The plants are the Oak, the Acacia, the Bay tree, Laurel, Gorse, the Ash tree. The element is Air. The Ruach.

PAROKETH

Below Tiphareth stretches a great veil called Paroketh which separates the planes of force and the planes of form. Metamorphosis takes place as the veil is penetrated and down going energy is braked and upgoing energy is accelerated. Polarity is also changed as the veil is passed through.

7 *Netzach* — Victory

The Occult or Hidden Intelligence. The God-Name is Tetragrammaton *Tzabaoth*, the Lord of Hosts. Netzach is *Nogah*, the Sphere of Venus. The Magic Image is a beautiful nude woman. This is the Kama. She is Hathor, Aphrodite, Venus, Freya, all Goddesses of Love. Netzach is Victory. This is Nike, Goddess of Victory. The color is Emerald Green. The symbols are the Lamp carried in the hand, the Girdle of Venus, the Laurel Wreath of Victory. The animals are the Raven, the Dove and the Inyx. The plants are the Rose and the Laurel. The minerals are Copper and Bronz. The perfume is Benzoin (a resin of a Sumatran tree but can be approximated by a mixture of bitter almond and oil of camphor).

8 *Hod* — Splendor

Also named Glory. The Resplendent Intelligence. God-Name: *Elohim Tzabaoth*, God of Hosts. Hod, Splendor or Glory, is *Kokab*, the Sphere of Mercury. This is Prana. It is the Conscious-Unconscious. It is Thought Energy. The Magic Image is Hermaphrodite. This is a Bi-Sexed Person. Hod is Thoth, Tahuti, Hanuman, Hermes, Mercury, Odin, Loki. The Instrument of Hermes is the Caduceus with twin serpents representing the Mercurial double current. The Masonic Apron is his. His are the Names and Versicles of Power. The color is Orange on the Queen Scale. The animals are those suggesting fleetness. Anubis and his Jackal belong here. The plant is Allium Moly, wild garlic. The mineral is Mercury, Quicksilver. The gem is the Opal. The perfume is Storax.

9 *Yesod* — Foundation

The Intelligence of Separative Influence. The God-Name is *Shaddai El Chai* (shahd-DOY el HOY), the Almighty Living God. Yesod is *Levannah*, the Sphere of Luna the Moon. This is the Libido. It is the Akasha. This is Flux and Reflux, Solidity, and Fluidity. It is the Aether of the Wise, the Astral Light, the Etheric World, the Etheric or Vital Body. Herein lies the Dual Manifestation of Truth. The Magic Image is a beautiful naked man, very strong. This is Atlas. It is Shu. Lord of the Firmament, Ganesha, Zeus, Jove, Jupiter as Foundation, Hermanubis as Lord of the Threshold, Terminus marking the boundary. Diana as

Goddess of the Moon is here, also Diana as phallic stone. Here too is ithyphallic Hermes, Pan, Priapus. All phallic gods might be attributed here. Yesod is the Altar, the Foundation of the Church. The animals are the Elephant, Tortoise and the Toad. The plants are Banyan, Mandrake, Ginseng, Damiana, Yohimba. All roots are sacred to Yesod as furnishing foundation. The mineral and gem of Yesod is Quartz. The Queen Scale color is Violet. All incenses and perfumes belong to Yesod but the particular perfume is Jasmine. The metal is Silver.

10   *Malkuth* — The Kingdom

The Corporeal Intelligence. The Name of God in Malkuth is *Adonai Malekh*, the Lord Who is King, or *Adonai ha Aretz*, Lord of Earth. Malkuth is the Gate: the Gate of Death, the Gate of Tears, the Gate of Prayer, the Gate of the Daughter of the Mighty Ones, the Gate of the Garden of Eden. Malkuth is the Princess, the Virgin who becomes Kallah the Bride. It is the He final of Tetragrammaton as twin and bride of the male child Vau. The Superior or Supernal Mother is Binah who reflects herself in Malkuth who is thus the Inferior Mother, Malkah the Queen, Mother Nature. Malkuth is the Sphere of the Earth which is also the Sphere of the Elements—Fire, Water, Air and Earth. The Sphinx is here as a composite of the four elements. The Magic Image is a Young Woman, throned and crowned. This is Persephone, the virgin earth. This is the lower Isis and Nephthys as Virgins, imperfect until impregnated. The Willow is the traditional tree of the neglected maiden. But the Daughter is the Mother as the Mother is the Daughter so Malkuth is also the Mother Goddess Lakshmi, Demeter, Ceres. The Queen Scale colors of Malkuth are Citrine, Russet, Olive and Black. The gem is Rock Crystal. The mineral is Salt. The Pomegranate is associated with Persephone. All cereals belong to Malkuth—Wheat, Oats, Corn, Rye, Maize, etc. The perfume is Dittany of Crete. The Lodge room Altar of the Double Cube belongs to Malkuth. Malkuth as Gate is the Door of the Church. The sandals of the Priest or Magician are Malkuth's. St. Luke and his Gospel is assigned here. Geomancy.

10X below the Earth is the Sphere of Pluto, the graveyard of the shells of the dead, *Cholom Yosodoth*. Also here is the Abode or Sphere of the Qlippoth.

THE THREE PILLARS

The Sephiroth are divided into three columns or pillars: the right-hand Pillar of Mercy, consisting of the second, fourth and seventh emanations; the left-hand Pillar of Severity, consisting of the third, fifth and eighth emanations; and the Middle Pillar of Mildness or Equilibrium, consisting of the first, sixth, ninth, and tenth emanations.

As we look at the Tree in Figure 3 on page 24 we see Binah, Geburah, and Hod on the left side, and Chokmah, Chesed, and Netzach on the right side. This is the way we view the Tree when we are using it to represent the Macrocosm, the greater universe of God. But when we use it to represent the Microcosm, the little universe of man—that is, our own being—we *back into it*, so that the Middle Pillar equates with the spine, the Pillar that contains Chokmah, Chesed and Netzach with the *left* side, and the Pillar that contains Binah, Geburah, and Hod with the *right* side.

The Pillar of Severity is negative or feminine and the Pillar of Mercy is positive or masculine. The line of the Lightning Flash, which indicates the successive development of the Sephiroth, zigzags from side to side. This indicates that the Sephiroth are successively positive, negative, and equilibrated.

The two Pillars of Mercy and Severity represent the positive and negative forces in nature, the active and the passive, the constructive and destructive. The middle Pillar of Mildness represents the equilibrium of the two opposing Pillars.

THE THREE TRIANGLES

Nine of the Sephiroth naturally group themselves into three triads or triangles as shown in Figure 4 on page 25. In each is a duad of opposite sexes or polarities, and a uniting intelligence. The masculine and feminine potencies are the two scales of a balance and the uniting Sephirah is the beam which joins them. Metheqela, balance, thus symbolizes the Triune, Trinity in Unity and the Unity, represented by the central point of the beam.

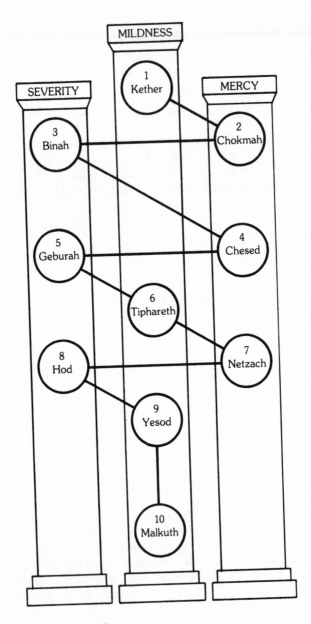

Figure 3. The Three Pillars.

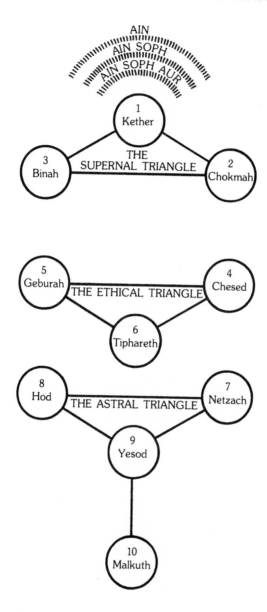

Figure 4. The Three Triangles.

In the Sephiroth there is a triple Trinity, the upper, middle and lower. Kether, Chokmah, and Binah form the upper Trinity, the Supernal Triad, the Supernals. This is called *Olahm Meushekal*, the Intellectual World. Chesed, Geburah and Tiphareth form the middle trinity, the Ethical Triad or Triangle, called *Olahm Morgash*, the Moral World. Netzach, Hod, and Yesod form the lower Trinity, the Astral Triad or Triangle, called *Olahm ha Nevetbau*, the World of Power and Stability.

Part II
The Way Back

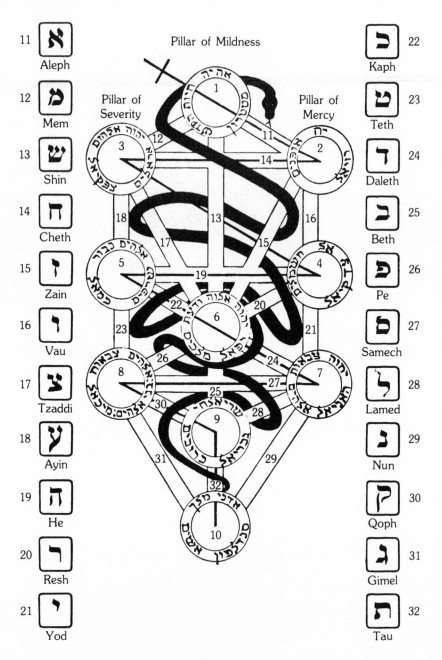

Figure 5. The Serpent of Wisdom *(Nehushtan)* on the Tree of Life.

The Path of the Serpent

THE TWENTY-TWO CONNECTING PATHS
OF THE TREE OF LIFE

32 Moon

The Perpetual Intelligence, Tau, Cross. The High Priestess, the
Priestess of the Silver Star. Levannah, Luna, Diana, Artemis, Hecate,
Chomse. Silver, pewter, aluminum. Moonstone, pearl, crystal. All
white and all night-blooming flowers. Hazel, almond, moonwort, iris,
watercress, Lily of the Valley (poisonous), Morning Glory, Wormwood
(Wormwood is one of the Bitter Herbs of the Bible—tops, flowers and
leaves are used—*strong stuff*, it contains Artemisia which is the basis
of Absinthe—its American cousin is Sagebrush). Camphor, menstrual
blood, virginal odors, Dittany of Crete. Dogs, especially hounds. Bow
and arrow. Memory. The Akashic Records. Virtue: discrimination.
Vice: indifference. Travel, domesticity, changefulness, divination by
dreams. Clairvoyance. Color: blue.

31 Aquarius

The Collective Intelligence. Gimel, camel. The Star, the Daughter of
the Firmament, the Dweller between the Waters. Aquarius, the
Waterbearer. Juno. Ganymede (Cupbearer beloved of Zeus). Stained
glass. Aerial flowers and plants and succulent (water-bearing) plants.
The peacock, Galbanum (a gum resin of Asian plant Ferula, it has a

peculiar odor—a more pleasant aroma which is occultly acceptable would be a mixture of dried rose petals and lavender). The Aspergillus (watersprinkler). The ankles. 11th House activities—hopes, wishes, friends, foster or step children, etc. Virtue: altruism. Vice: Argumentation. Platonic love, friendship. Astrology. "I know." Color: purple. Tristitia in Geomancy.

30   Capricorn

The Exciting Intelligence. Qoph, back of the head. The Medulla Oblongata, Seat of the Instincts. The Devil, the Lord of the Gates of Matter, the Child of the Forces of Time. Capricorn, the Goat, the Sea Goat, the Sea Monster. Priapus, Pan, Set, Bacchus, Khem, Kundalini, Kernunnos. The phallus, the Lingam, the Yoni. Hemp, Cannabis, Marijuana. Orchis root (Orchis is a terrestrial orchid of the temperate zone, name from the Greek ORCHIS, testicle. Plant with roots like testicles.) Pussy Willow bark, Night Blooming Cereus (flowers and stems), ginseng, Damiana (plant common in California, Texas and Mexico), Yohimba (from Africa), Saw Palmeto berries (dwarf palmetto of Florida) are powerful Aphrodisiacs. The oyster. The ass. Musk, civet, semen. The knees. The sex drive, the libido, the generative power, the creative force. Virtue: diplomacy. Vice: deceitfulness. 10th House activities—occupation, honors, fame, etc. "I use." Color: indigo. Geomantic Carcer.

29   Pisces

The Constituting Intelligence. Nun, Fish. The waning moon, the Ruler of Flux and Reflux, the Child of the Sons of the Mighty. Pisces, the Fishes. Neptune, Poseidon, Anubis. All water plants and single cell organisms. The jackal, the dolphin, the crayfish, the beetle, the lobster. Ambergris. The Magic Mirror. All narcotics. Hypnotism, mysticism, psychic sensitivity. Mediumship. Pearl, aquamarine, bloodstone, Virtue: sympathy. Vice: worry. The feet. The Dark Night of the Soul. 12th House activities—Self undoing, confinement, limitations, enemies, etc. "I believe." Color: Crimson. Scrying, crystal gazing, hydromancy. Geomantic Laetitia.

28   Aries

The Intelligence of Will. Lamed, ox goad. The Emperor, Sun of the Morning, Chief Among the Mighty. Aries, the Ram. Men-thu, Shiva,

Ares, Mars, Minerva, Athena. Ruby, garnet. Tiger Lily, geranium. All male leaders of herds. Dragon's Blood, musk. The horns. The burin (an instrument for engraving furrows in metal such as initials to identify maker or owner, same sense as using branding iron). Power of consecrating things. Leadership. The head. Alchemical sulphur, the male fiery energy. Orb surmounted by Maltese Cross. Virtue: determination. Vices: officiousness, egotism, rashness. 1st House activities—nativity, personality, disposition. Ability to rule and to lead. "I am." Color: Scarlet. Geomantic Puer.

27 Sagittarius

The Renewing Intelligence. Samech, a Prop. Temperance, the Daughter of the Reconcilers, the Bringer-Forth of Life. Sagittarius, the Archer, the Centaur. Apollo and Artemis as Hunters, Diana as Archer, Nephthys. Jacinth (the gem hyacinth when pure orange in color). Plants: rush, aloes. Horse, dog. Frankincense. The Arrow. Transmutation, metamorphosis, promotion, demotion. Form to force (ascending), force to form (descending). Alchemy, change of internal structure, thus of outer appearance. Virtue: directness. Vice: wastefulness. Hips and Thighs. 9th House activities—long journeys, higher education, intuition, etc. "I see." Color: blue. Geomantic Acquisitio.

26 Mercury

The Serving or Administrative Intelligence. Pe, Mouth. The Magician, the Magus of Power, the Juggler with the Secret of the Universe. The planet Mercury. Thoth, Tahuti, Hermes, Mercury, Hanuman, Herne. Quicksilver. The opal, the agate. Lilac, palm, licorice, anise, dill, caraway, fennel, horehound, ginseng, wild garlic (Moly). Ibis, ape, dog. Mastic (resin of European tree, Mastic, smells like varnish), Mace (dried covering of nutmeg), Storax (gum resin of Storax tree). The Wand. The Caduceus. Mastery of sciences and languages, gift of tongues, miracles of healing. Nervous system. Dexterity. Intelligence. The Messenger. Virtue: truthfulness. Vices: dishonesty, falsehood. Color: yellow.

25 Sun

The Natural Intelligence. Beth, house. The Sun, Lord of the Fire of the World. Sol, the Sun. Helios, Apollo, Surya, Ra. Gold. All golden colored stones. Angelica, bay, camomile, marigold, peony, sunflower, heliotrope. Lion, hawk. Frankincense. The circulatory system. Power of acquiring wealth. Power, authority, life. Virtue: generosity. Vice: pride. "In the Sun is the Secret of the Spirit." Color: orange.

24   Venus

The Imaginative Intelligence. Daleth, door. The Empress, the Daughter of the Mighty Ones. The planet Venus. Aphrodite, Venus, Freya, Hathor, Lolita. Copper, brass, bronze. Emerald, turquoise. Myrtle, rose, clover, orange blossom, columbine, daisy, peach, plum, all sweet smelling flowers. Sparrow, dove, swan, cow, sow. Sandalwood, vanilla, all soft, voluptuous odors. The girdle, love philtres. The venous system. Love, beauty, sociability. Virtue: graciousness. Vices: lust, unchastity. Color: green.

23   Gemini

The Intelligence of the House of Influence. Ayin, eye. The Lovers, the Children of the Voice, the Oracle of the Mighty Gods. Crowley says this Tarot card should be titled "The Brothers." Gemini, the Twins. Castor and Pollux, Apollo the Diviner, Janus, various twin and hybrid deities. Alexandrite, tourmaline, Icelandic spar. Bay leaves, orchids, peyote, hybrid plants. Magpie. Mule and all hybrid animals. Wormwood. The tripod. The Power of Bi-Location. Astral travel. The power of prophecy (to prophesy: inhale fumes of Bay Leaves burned on Charcoal in a Censer). Virtue: versatility. Vice: changeableness. Hands and arms, upper respiratory tract. 3rd House activities— studies, lower education, short journeys, brothers and sisters, neighbors, etc. "I think." Color: orange. Albus.

22   Mars

The Faithful Intelligence. Kaph, closed hand, fist. The Tower, the House of God, the Lord of the Hosts of the Mighty. The planet Mars. Horus, Ares, Mars. Iron, steel. Ruby, garnet, any red stone. Briony, garlic, gentian, mustard, horseradish, onion, rue. Horse, bear, wolf. Pepper, Dragon's Blood, gunpowder, burning sulphur. Spear, sword, chain, scourge. Works of wrath and vengeance. The muscular system. Aggression. Virtue: energetic defense of right. Vices: wrath, cruelty. Color: red.

21   Virgo

The Stable Intelligence. Yod, hand. The hand is a polite equivalent, the real meaning is the male spermatozoon which the Yod pictures. The Hermit, the Prophet of the Eternal, the Magus of the Voice of Power. Virgo, the Virgin, Isis as Virgin, Attis, Adonis, the Gopi Girls, the Lord of Yoga. The Virgin, the Anchorite, all nuns, all monks, priests and celibates by choice, any solitary person or animal, virile force reserved. The peridot. The narcissus, the snowdrop. Dittany of Crete. Sheaf of wheat, loaf of bread. Power of invisibility. Parthenogenesis, reproduction by development of unfertilized egg, does happen in some crustaceans, insects and worms. Navel and bowels. Virtue: analysis. Vice: criticism. 6th House activities—servants, food, clothing, sickness, small animals, etc. "I Analyze." Color: yellowish green. Conjunctio.

20   Jupiter

The Intelligence of Conciliation. Resh, head or face. The Wheel of Fortune, the Lord of the Forces of Life. The planet Jupiter. Amoun-Ra, Brahma, Indra, Zeus, Jove, Jupiter. Santa Claus, the Benevolent Giver of Gifts. Tin. Amethyst, lapis lazuli. Balm, chervil, hyssop, oak, sage, dahlia, fig, all evergreens. Saffron (aromatic pungent dried stigmas of a species of Crocus with purple flowers), Turmeric. The scepter. Power of acquiring ascendency. The digestive system. Virtue: generosity. Vices: gluttony, bigotry. Religion. Jurisprudence. Color: violet.

19   Libra

The Intelligence of the Secret of All Spiritual Activities. (The entire secret of the Occult is the knowledge of equilibrium.) He, window. Justice, the Daughter of the Lords of Truth, the Ruler of the Balance. Justesse, the Act of Adjustment. Libra, the Scales. Maat, Themis, Vulcan, Yama. The Emerald. The aloe, the elephant. Galbanum (see Path 31). The scales, the balance, the cross of equilibrium, the circled cross. The reins (region of the kidneys), the liver, the kidneys. Psychic sensitivity. Partnership. Virtue: fairness. Vice: reading other people's mail, going through others' drawers and closets, peeping into others' privacy. 7th House activities—marriage, partnership, contracts, etc. "I balance." Puella. Color: yellowish green.

18   Scorpio

The Intelligence of Probation or Trial. Teth, serpent. Death, the Child of the Great Transformers, the Lord of the Gate of Death. Scorpio, the Scorpion. Typhon, Kephra, Kundalini. The Snakestone. The scorpion, the serpent, the eagle. Cactus. Benzoin, a balsam gum resin from a tree of the Storax family, its American cousin is the laurel. The genitalia. Creativity. The Oedipus complex. Virtue: minding one's own business. Vice: sarcasm. "I desire." Color: greenish-blue. Rubeus.

17   Cancer

The Disposing Intelligence. Tzaddi, fish hook. The Chariot, the Child of the Powers of the Waters, the Lord of the Triumph of Light. Cancer, the Crab. Khephra, Hormakhu, Apollo the Charioteer. Amber. Water lily, lotus. The crab, the turtle. Onycha, burnt seashell, good substitute is myrrh. The power of casting enchantments. Breasts, bosom, lower lungs, stomach. Nutrition. Virtue: concern for others' welfare. Vice: inertia. 4th House activities—home, property, end of life. "I feel." Color: amber. Populus and Via.

16   Taurus

The Triumphant and Eternal Intelligence. Vau, nail. The Hierophant, the Magus of the Eternal. Taurus, the Bull. Osiris, Apis the Bull, Shiva as Sacred Bull. Topaz. Daisy, mallow. All bovines, cattle, bison, yak. Storax or Dittany of Crete. The labor of preparation. The establishment. The secret of physical strength. Success in hatha yoga. Neck and shoulders. Virtue: determination. Vice: greed. 2nd House activities—possessions, finances. "I have." Color: red-orange. Admissio.

15   Leo

The Luminous Intelligence. Zain, sword. Strength, the Daughter of the Flaming Sword. Leo, the Lion. Horus, Pasht, Mau, Demeter borne by lions. Tiger eye, cat's eye. Sunflower. All large members of the cat family. Olibanum (frankincense). Power of training wild beasts. The heart, the back. Rulership. Virtue: courage. Vice: egoism, arrogance. 5th House activities—children, love affiars, speculation. "I will." Color: greenish-yellow. Fortuna Major and Fortuna Minor.

14   Saturn

The Uniting Intelligence. Cheth, fence or field. The Universe, the World, the Great One of the Night of Time. The planet Saturn. Ohapsi, Kronos, Saturn. Lead. Ash, cypress, yew, nightshade, aconite (wolfbane), comfrey. Crocodile. Onyx, Jet. Asafoetida, scammony. The sickle. Works of malediction and death. The bony system, the skeleton. Old people, antiques, land. Time and timepieces. Limitation. Safety. Karma. Virtue: stability. Vice: sluggishness. Color: indigo.

13   Fire

The Scintillating or Fiery Intelligence. Shin, tooth. The Last Judgement or the Angel, the Spirit of the Primal Fire. Tejas, an upright red equilateral triangle. Agni, Yama, Iacchus as Lord of Ecstasy. The fire opal. The red poppy, hibiscus, nettle. The salamanders. Frankincense. The incense burner. Pyromancy. Aspiration. Ecstasy. The South. The Path of the Ascension of Christ. The Path of the Descent of the Holy Ghost. Michael the Archangel. St. Mark and his Gospel. Color: red.

12   Water

The Intelligence of Transparency. Mem, water. The Hanged Man, the Spirit of the Mighty Waters. Apas, a Silver Cresent. The chalice, the cup. Soma, Neptune, Poseidon. Osiris as Hanged Man, Jesus as Hanged Man. Beryl, aquamarine. Lotus and all water plants. Myrrh, a gum resin. Crystal gazing. Hydromancy. Talismans. The sacramental wine. Nymphs, undines. The West. Gabriel the Archangel. St. John and his Gospel. Color: blue.

11   Air

The Pure Intelligence. Aleph, ox. The Fool, the Holy Innocent. Vayu, a Blue Disc. The dagger. The fan. Hoor-par-kraat, the Child Jesus, the Holy Innocents. Aspen tree, Spanish Moss, peppermint, spearmint, all aerial plants. The butterfly. The topaz. Galbanum (see Path 31). The rose by its odor is associated with Air. Pranayama. Divination. Sylphs, fairies. The East. Raphael the Archangel. St. Matthew Gospel, *not* Matthew the Apostle. Color: yellow.

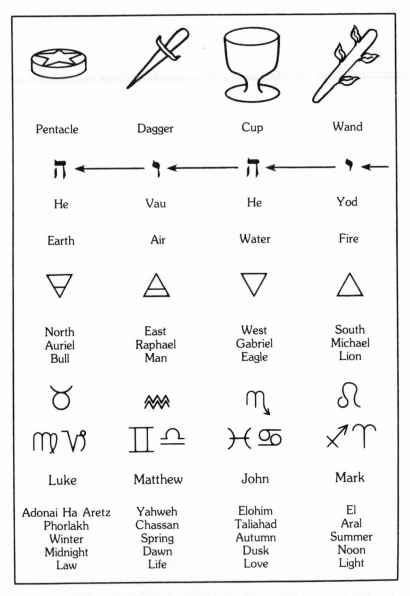

Pentacle	Dagger	Cup	Wand
He	Vau	He	Yod
Earth	Air	Water	Fire
North Auriel Bull	East Raphael Man	West Gabriel Eagle	South Michael Lion
Luke	Matthew	John	Mark
Adonai Ha Aretz Phorlakh Winter Midnight Law	Yahweh Chassan Spring Dawn Life	Elohim Taliahad Autumn Dusk Love	El Aral Summer Noon Light

Figure 6. The Formula of Tetragrammaton. Study these symbols and internalize them. These symbols will help you understand the rituals, for they illustrate the path to wisdom and consciousness. The trick is, the symbols are very simple—what is the greater concept they stand for?

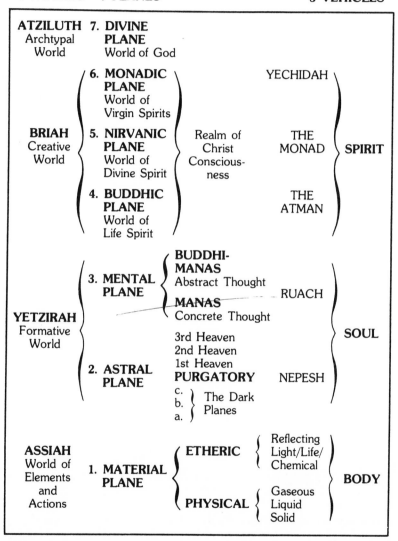

Figure 7. Diagram of the universal set-up. Each of us is a microcosm that reflects the macrocosm, but not until we *know* it! How does the universe of the self fit into the greater universe? Study this diagram—it will help you understand the scope of yourself in a greater awareness.

Part III
Rituals of Return

Priestess of the Silver Star

Required Reading: *The Mystical Qabalah*, by Dion Fortune. *The Finding of the Third Eye*, by Vera Stanley Alder.

Prerequisite: Knowledge of the influence of the Moon in the twelve Signs of the Zodiac and in the twelve Houses of the Horoscope. Ability to perform a Tarot Divination.

Time: New Moon.

On stand against eastern wall is a statue or picture of a muscular unclothed man such as Atlas or the seated Hermes with white candles on either side. On Altar (two black cubes, boxes, each with one side inwardly hinged, one cube on top of the other) in center of room are the four Magical Instruments in their proper places, Rod or Wand in the south, Cup with white wine in the west, Dagger in the east and Pentacle, Disk or Coin in the north. Also on the Altar are white or pastel flowers with a Tau cross (a T-shaped cross) hidden among them, a consecrated Kamea of the Moon and Tarot Atu II, the High Priestess. The Pillars of Hermes are west of the Altar, the black pillar of Boaz (Boaz means strong, power, might) to the north, the white pillar of Joachin (yah-kah-een, meaning "He shall establish") to the south. Chair, facing east, is west of Pillars, ritual book on stand to right of chair. On stand against south wall is a thurible (a swinging incense burner) with charcoal tablets, a container of dittany of crete incense, an ash tray, a cigarette lighter or a packet of matches.

Clothed only in robe, girdle and sandals, enter room (hereinafter referred to as the Temple), salute Altar by raising right arm, hand of which is a fist with thumb between forefinger and middle finger (knuckles upward) to an angle of forty-five degrees, left hand flat on left breast, pause, then hands returned to side, take three steps forward, bow low from the waist, straighten. Go deosil (clockwise, turning to the right) to south, take lighter or matches and ignite charcoal, go by way of west and north to east, light candles, go to south, return lighter or matches to stand in south, continue to chair in west, sit. Pause, then read aloud:

I am sitting in Malkuth (Mahl-kooth) *of Assiah* (uh-sigh-yuh) *looking through the Portals of Hermes, the Portals of Solomon, upon Path Thirty-Two of the Tree of Life, the path that leads from Malkuth to Yesod* (yay-sode). *Malkuth, the Kingdom, is the Tenth Path of which the Sepher Yetzirah* (seff-er yet-zye-ruh), *the Book of Formation, says "The Tenth Path is called the Corporeal Intelligence and is so called because it forms the very body which is formed beneath the whole order of the worlds and the increment of them." This saying, as many others in Theurgy, I do not as yet fully understand. I hope to, and I shall some day. On the Noble Eight-fold Path of the Lord Buddha this path is Right Viewpoint. The hope and the will to attain—is this a right viewpoint for me? The Virtue here is Discrimination. Do I discriminate rightly? Do I choose wisely?* [Pause in self-examination.] *The Vice here is Indifference. To what am I indifferent?* [Pause.] *How is this a vice?* [Pause.] *Here in Malkuth, I need help, oh, how I need help!*

Stand and pray:

Adonai Melehk (ah-doh-NOH-ee may-leck), *Lord who is King! Adonai ha Aretz* (ah-doh-NOH-ee hah ah-retz), *Lord of Earth! May I stand firmly upon the solid and sure rock of Right Doctrine and so have the Right Viewpoint of thy Kingdom! I ask for the blessing and assistance of the holy angel Sandalphon in obtaining and maintaining true discrimination, may I avoid sluggishness and indifference, may I have the opportunities to develop, to have and to hold, the qualities of strength and endurance, stability and practicality, to the end that I may perform the Great Work and so find myself to be one with Thee! Amen.*

Sit. Enter the Silence by placing both hands palm down on thighs or knees, bowing head, closing eyes and whispering:

In the Name of the Lord of the Universe who works in Silence and whom naught but the Silence can express, I enter the Silence.

Then become absolutely quiet, utterly still. After a while, open eyes, take Ritual Book and read aloud:

The Thirty-Second Path is before me. I desire to tread it, my desire is to experience it. But in order to do so I must be worthy, well-qualified, and duly and truly prepared. The Ritual Book of Magic tells me the worthiness of the candidate for Initiation into the mysteries is assumed. It is left to the Invisible Masters of the Inner Orders to do the judging. Suffice to know that if the candidate be unworthy he (she) will not experience the expansion of consciousness, the mental-emotional-spiritual going into "high gear," and a beginning of another and higher way of life which is true Initiation. Am I worthy? [Pause long enough to do some sincere soul-searching.] *Am I qualified?* [Pause to consider **how** you are qualified.] *Am I duly and truly prepared?* [Here review the Prerequisites of this Rite as if some authority or teacher were giving you an examination.] *The Sepher Yetzirah says, "The Thirty-Second Path is the Perpetual Intelligence because it rules the movements of the Moon according to their constitution and perfects all the revolutions of the Zodiac and the form of their judgements."*

Stand. Go to Pillars, give Sign of Enterer [Hands in front, palms together in attitude of prayer, head slightly bowed, bend slightly forward from waist while advancing left foot forward a pace. Hold this posture for a couple of seconds.] Then step deliberately through the portal and proceed to Altar, genuflect, go deosil to south, cast incense upon the glowing charcoal and cense the Altar with three swings left, three swings right, three swings forward, replace Thurible, go to west, face and approach Altar, take Tarot card, hold it high and say:

Priestess of the Silver Star! Initiatrix into the Mysteries! In your lap is the mystic scroll of the Akashic Records, the Memory of Nature! On your breast is the equal-armed cross. I aspire to the ability to unroll and read that scroll! I aspire to achieve the balance of the four elements of my being so as also to wear the equal-armed cross! Lend me thine aid!

Replace card. Touch each of the four Instruments, say:

> *Let Rod have rulership of right*
> > *To guide me on the Path of Light.*
> *Let Cup be charged with competence*
> > *To fill me with benevolence.*
> *Let Dagger be sharp and ever keen*
> > *To save me from all things unclean.*
> *Let Disk be adequate and sure*
> > *To keep me faithful and secure.*

Again hold the Tarot card high and say:

The Priestess of the Silver Star thus instructs the Candidate, "Know that the Holy Guardian Angel is attained by self-sacrifice and discipline. Purity is to live only to the Highest; and the Highest is the ALL. Be thou as Artemis to Pan."

Pause in contemplation of the High Priestess' words. Replace Tarot card. Then touch the Kamea of the Moon and say;

O Lady of the Night! Diana! Luna! Artemis! Levannah! Maiden of Many Names! Great thou art and greatly to be praised! May your words sink deeply into my soul! May I share your Virtue of Contentment. May I, like you, go my way serenely. The Magic Powers you endow are Clairvoyance and Divination by Dreams. I would be greatly honored to receive these gifts from you!

Kneel and adore in silence. Then stand and say:

The Sin of this Path is Indolence. Indolence! A polite word for laziness. I vow henceforth to avoid this sin. The Vice of this Path is Idleness. I vow henceforth to avoid this vice. So here and now let willing hands be dedicated. [Spit on right hand.] *Blessed be the hand put forth with might.* [Spit on left hand.] *Blessed be the hand put forth in meaning.* [Rub hands together vigorously.] *Blessed be what I must* do with might and meaning that my hands hold the harvest of my highest hopes.

Take Cup, hold it high, and say:

The pale wine of the New Moon.

Spill a little wine onto the flowers, saying:

I offer fermented juice of the pale grape to the Lady of the Night.

Discover the Tau Cross. Say:

What's this? A gift from the lady! A Tau! What can it mean? Thank you, my Lady! I drink to you!

Drink the wine. Replace Cup. Examine Tau Cross and say:

This token from the Lady is a Tau. Tau is a Hebrew letter. It means cross. Cross! She has an equal-armed cross on her bosom. Cross! What can it mean? Perhaps she is telling me something. Perhaps she is showing me the way! The way...of the cross...leads...home. The way of the cross leads home!

Clutching the cross to your bosom, dance deosil around Altar, singing or chanting three times:

> *The way of the cross leads home!*
> *The way of the cross leads home!*
> *It is sweet to know*
> *As I onward go*
> *The way of the cross leads home.*

Finish dance in the west. Sit, enter the Silence. After a while, perform Closing Exercises of Temple Rite thusly: Seated, make the Qabalistic Cross by touching forehead saying *THINE*, touch center of chest saying *IS THE KINGDOM*, touch right shoulder saying *AND THE POWER*, touch left shoulder saying *AND THE GLORY*, hands together in attitude of prayer, fingers and palms together and touching, bow head saying *FOREVER AND EVER. AMEN.* Then, head still bowed and hands still together, intone *HUA* three times as Hooooo-Ahhhh! On final intonation stand, raising head and at the same time shoving the hands upward over head, then outward and downward as a diver coming up out of the water, letting the "ah" of the final HUA become an explosion or a bark with sharp expulsion of breath. Immediately give the sign of Silence. Press tip of right forefinger firmly against closed lips while mentally saying:

> *To will, to know, to dare and to keep silent!*
> *Love is the law, love under will.*

Silently circumambulate widdershine (counter-clockwise, turning to the left) the Temple three times. Stop in the west. Bow, take three steps backward, salute Altar as in opening. The Rite is finished.

● ● ●

Wear the Tau Cross on your person until the Full Moon. Sleep with the Kamea of the Moon under your pillow every night and remember to record your dreams every morning until Full Moon. Practice various forms of visualization and various techniques of inducing Clairvoyance every day until Full Moon, but do not permit your Psychic Ability to become dependent on any physical thing.

The Water Bearer

Prerequisite: Ability to erect and delineate an astrological natal chart. Performance of the Rite of Path Thirty-Two.

Time: Moon waxing in Aquarius.

On stand against eastern wall is a statue or picture of Hermes or Mercury or Tarot Atu I, the Magician, with white or lavender candles on either side. On floor or footstool before this is a potted plant with an artificial butterfly or bird perched on its top. On Altar are Tarot Atu XVII, the Star, in center, Cup with water in west and Dagger in east. Roses or aspen leaves or spanish moss or sprigs of peppermint are scattered over Altar or may be in low vases north and south. Hidden under the Cup is a small piece of parchment or heavy paper on which has been drawn in black ink the symbol of Aquarius and the Hebrew letter Gimel with this message written, "Use all thine energy to rule thy thought." Pillars west of Altar and chair west of them. On stand by chair are Ritual Book, horoscope blank, ephemeris of the current year, Tables of Houses, work sheet, watch or clock and pen or pencil. A small electric fan or air circulator to create a gentle breeze would be most appropriate. Thurible with charcoal, lighter or matches and ashtray and container of incense on stand in south. Incense: galbanum if possible, otherwise a mixture of rose petals and lavender. This Rite is to be performed Sky-clad, which means naked.

If possible enter Temple from the north or the west. Upon entering, salute the Altar by raising right arm, hand of which is a fist with thumb between forefinger and middle finger, to an angle of forty-five degrees, left hand flat on left breast. Then, hands returned to side, take three steps forward, stop, bow low from the waist, straighten. Go deosil to south, take lighter or matches and ignite charcoal, go by way of west and north to east, light candles, go to south, return lighter or matches to stand, continue to west to north to east to south to west while saying aloud:

Round and round about this Temple I draw a magic circle, a magic circle of light!

Visualize a circle of fire surrounding the Temple. Now standing before chair and facing Altar, make another circle: Beginning with right arm stretched straight upward, forefinger extended, other fingers clasped to palm by thumb, draw a clock as a circle of fire with sweeping motion of arm from up to right to down to left to up, saying:

Round and round about this temple I draw a magic circle, a magic circle of light!

Then draw another fiery circle from down front to up to back to down, saying:

Round and round about this Temple I draw a magic circle, a magic circle of light!

Then say:

Three magic circles have I drawn, that of Space, that of Time and that of Events. Without are other worlds, but this is mine. This is mine! I am its creator, I am its ruler. And so mote it be.

Sit. Facing east, spine straight, both feet flat on the floor and slightly apart, hands resting palm down on thighs or knees, chin up, eyes closed, repeat aloud many, many times:

All the power that ever was, all the power that ever will be, is here right now.

Say it several times slowly, softly but distinctly. Then begin saying it louder and more rapidly, gradually increasing the volume and tempo until you are shouting it excitedly at great speed. When you feel power surging within and around you say:

Power is available to me by the simple act of my acceptance. I accept. I accept. I accept.

Take seven deep breaths, inhaling through the nose, holding the breath a little longer than usual, exhaling audibly through the open mouth. Now stand, raise both arms in adoration, head thrown back, and intone three times:

IAO! IAO! IAO! [Lips bared, jaws slightly apart, deepen or lower voice, saying *"Eeeeee!"*; mouth wide open, say *"Ahhhh!"*; purse mouth in open circle saying *"Ohhhh!"*]

Lower left arm. Perform the Qabalistic Cross. Immediately give the Sign of the Enterer: Hands still together in the attitude of prayer, head still bowed, bend or bow slightly at the waist while advancing left foot forward a step. Short pause, maintaining pose. Then circumambulate to north to east to south, cast incense onto the glowing charcoal in the Thurible and cense Altar with three swings left, three swings right, three swings forward, return Thurible, go to west, sit. Enter the Silence. After a while, read aloud:

I am sitting in Malkuth of Assiah, looking through the Portals upon Path Thirty-One that leads from Malkuth to Hod (Hod rhymes with lode and road). *The Sepher Yetzirah says, "The Thirty-First Path is the Collecting Intelligence, and it is so-called because Astrologers deduce from it the judgement of the Stars and of the Celestial Signs and the perfection of their science according to the rules of their resolutions." I am an Astrologer. To demonstrate this I shall set up a chart for this very minute.* [Do so quickly but accurately.] *Moon is in Aquarius now and the Path before me and this Rite are dedicated and attributed to Aquarius. Whereas most Astronomers and many Astrologers declare the Age of Aquarius to be a long time in the future, as far as I am concerned I'm in the Age of Aquarius right now.* [Stand.] *The Age of Aquarius! The Age of Freedom! Free from the shackles of time and space! Free from the limitations of the physical! Free from the oppressions of false theologies, power-structure ideologies, hypocritical moralities! Freedom to be! Freedom to become! Freedom to do! Freedom to live and let live, to love and let love! Do what thou wilt shall be the whole of the law, for love is the law, love under will!*

Dance deosil lightly and joyously around Altar singing "The Age of Aquarius" from "Hair" or any other light and airy song such as "Funiculi Funicula." Finish dance in the west, face Altar, take the Tarot card, hold it high and say:

Daughter of the Firmament! Dweller between the waters! Holy thou art, pure and innocent! You see clearly for your eyes are not dimmed by self-interest. I pray for the Gift of Spiritual Insight.

Replace card on Altar, kneel and say:

Uranus! Lord of Magic! When time began to rule you withdrew into the far recesses of Timelessness and Spacelessness. From that vantage point you see clearly, oh so clearly. Endow me, I pray, with clearness of vision, give me realization of the possibilities, the human potential, both in myself and in others.

Pause in yearning. Stand. Touch the Tarot card, saying:

This is the Imagination of Nature. This is Aquarius the Waterbearer. I see the Waterbearer as a giant male figure, feet wide apart, in his arms a great urn or vessel from which he is pouring cool, clear water upon parched dry earth. [Vividly visualize.] *I see the Waterbearer as Ganymede the Cupbearer, the beautiful boy beloved of Zeus.* [Vividly visualize.] *I see the Waterbearer as Aeolus, God the Winds.* [Vividly visualize.] *I see the Waterbearer as Juno, Lady of Air.* [Vividly visualize.] *I see the Waterbearer as the Star of the Tarot.*

Gaze at the card for a moment, then kneel, imitating her pose. Hold this pose for a moment, then stand, take Cup from Altar, circumambulate deosil, carrying the Cup, watering the plant in the east, saying:

I, too, am a Waterbearer.

Continue circumambulation to west, replace Cup. In doing so discover the parchment or paper. Say:

What's this? A note! Perhaps a message? What is it? The Symbol of Aquarius. The Hebrew letter Gimel. And these words, "Use all thine energy to rule thy thought." Hmmmm! Use all thine energy to rule thy thought. The Hebrew letter Gimel means Camel. This must be a signature or a clue or a key. The number Gimel is three. The third Sephira of the Tree of Life is Binah (Bee-nuh), the Water above the Firmament. A Camel is a pack animal, a means of transportation, associated with deserts, dry places where there is little or no water. And the Camel is supposed to be able to go great distances without water. I presume he takes long drinks and carries his water with him. A Waterbearer! Here I am on the Thirty-First Path, behind me is Malkuth. Before me is Hod which is on the Pillar of Severity headed by Binah. In order to bring the Waters of Truth from Binah above to Malkuth below I must use all my energy to rule my thought. [Pause to comprehend.] *Thank you, Great Ones beyond and behind my being!* [Pause.] *The Vice of this Path is Argumentation. This I promise to avoid. The Virtue of this Path is Altruism. This I promise to cultivate.*

Dance again deosil around the Altar, singing the same song. Finish dance in the west. Sit. Enter the Silence. After a while, perform Closing Exercises of Temple Rite as given at end of Rite of Path Thirty-Two.

The Way of the Mystic

Required Reading: *Mysticism* by Evelyn Underhill.

Prerequisite: Rite of Path Thirty-One.

Time: At or near Midnight with waning Moon in Pisces.

On stand against easten wall is a statue or picture of Venus or Tarot Atu III, the Empress, with green candles and matches. On center of Altar is a goldfish bowl or aquarium with two live fish and green water plants, Cup with water in west, a bitter herb such a Wormwood or Water Cress and a container of salt and Pentacle or Coin in the north. Scattered on top of Altar are sea shells and sea weed or water plants with a natural or cultured pearl among them and a dried or artificial scarab or beetle or crayfish in the east. Also on Altar is Tarot Atu XVIII, the Waning Moon, Pillars east of Altar. Ritual Book on stand by chair in west. Incense: myrrh.

Robed, hooded, girded and sandaled, enter Temple, salute Altar, go by north to east, light candles, go to south, ignite charcoal, go to west, sit with hands folded together with thumb tips touching opposite palm,

head bowed, hood almost covering face. Long pause. Then raise
hood, take Ritual Book and read aloud:

*I am sitting in Malkuth of Assiah, looking upon Path Twenty-Nine of
the Tree of Life, the path that leads from Malkuth to Netzach.
Immediately before me is water with fishes and water plants. Beyond
are two towers. The Sepher Yetzirah says, "The Twenty-Ninth Path
is the Constituting Intelligence and is so called because it constitutes
the substance of creation in pure darkness which is that darkness
spoken of in Scripture, Job 38-9, 'and thick darkness a swaddling band
for it.'" To Path Twenty-Nine is ascribed the Zodiacal Sign of Pisces
the Fishes, the Hebrew letter NUN which means Fish, and Tarot Atu
XVIII, the Waning Moon.*

> *Here is a quest that calls me,*
> *This night when I am lone,*
> *The need to go where the ways divide*
> *The known from the unknown.*

Stand. Circumambulate deosil slowly to south, saying:

*This is the Path of the Imponderable Forces of Nature. Here I find the
place, the tenuous rim where the Seen grows dim and the Sightless
hides its face.*

Cast incense upon the glowing charcoal and cense the Altar saying:

> [Censing left] *Evohe! (ay-voh-AY-ee) Evohe! Poseidon!*
>   *(poh-SIGH-don)*
> [Censing right] *Evohe! (ay-voh-AY-ee) Evohe! Neptune!*
> [Censing front] *Evohe! (ay-voh-AY-ee) Evohe! Lord of the Deep!*

Replace Thurible. Go to west, face Altar, take Tarot Atu XVIII, hold it
high and say:

*Ruler of Flux and Reflux! Child of the Sons of the Mighty! Older than
night or day yet younger than the babe new born! Ever changing yet
ever the same! Male and female, both and neither! Father who is the
mother, mother who is the father! Parent who is the child, child who is
the parent! Reveal to me your Mystery!*

Lower card and gaze intently at it for a moment. Then say:

*It is night. The waning moon is overhead. Tears are dropping. Below
is water. Life in the form of a crayfish (beetle) is emerging out of the*

water onto a much-trodden path. Bitter plants grow beside the water. The path traverses cultivated fields until it passes between two towers of nameless mystery, beyond which is a dark foreboding forest and high dark menacing mountains. A wolf and a jackal are sitting at the base of the towers, baying the moon. [Pause.] Listen! I can hear them! The howling of wild animals—a beast of prey and a scavenger of rotting carcasses! Something—or somebody—is hiding behind a tower, lurking there, furtively watching me, perhaps waiting for me. Dark shadows beyond the towers are moving stealthily—now still as death—now darting quickly, now still again, now moving so very slowly. It's getting darker, the moon gives no light. [Close eyes and vividly visualize the scene. Pause. A "horror of great darkness" will come upon you.] Anubis! Watcher at midnight! Jackal-headed god of Khem who stands upon the threshold! This is the threshold of life, this is the threshold of death! Lend me thine aid! Go before me and lead the way!

Replace the Tarot card on the Altar. Circumambulate deosil while saying:

There is a budding morrow in midnight. Let the Illusion of the World pass over me, unheeded, as I go from the Midnight to the Morning.

Return to the west, face Altar and say:

The Vice of this Path is Worry. May my evergrowing, ever-deepening, ever-abiding faith in the Great Ones beyond and behind my being prevent me from indulging in this Vice. The Virtue of this Path is Sympathy. May I have sympathy like that of the Angels of Heaven! [Put a pinch of salt in the water in the Cup.] Salt are the tears and bitter is the taste of the Dark Night of the Soul! [Eat the bitter herb. Drink the salted water.] Yet how splended is the adventure [find and pick up the pearl] for in the midst of suffering and pain can be found the Pearl of Great Price! [Kiss the pearl and return it. Salute the figure on the stand in the east by raising right arm to a forty-five degree angle.] Hail the Morning Star!

Sit. Enter the Silence. Perform Closing Exercises of Temple Rite.

The Secret Flame

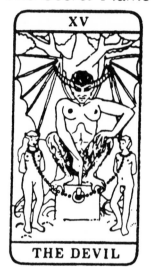

XV

THE DEVIL

Prerequisite: Rite of Path Twenty-Nine.

Time: Waxing Moon in Capricorn. If possible, on a Saturday.

Black Pillar in northeast corner of room. White Pillar in southeast corner. Before black Pillar, facing southwest, is stand with statue or picture of Hermes or Mercury or Tarot Atu I, the Magician, with lavender candles. Altar in center of room, so placed that its eastern side faces the northeast corner of the room. For the centerpiece on the Altar use your ingenuity in devising a "Secret Flame." This may be a miniature red globed oil lamp or a small candle in a ruby-red glass bowl. Put two oval or round stones beside it, or two hickory nuts. On Altar are the four Magical Instruments in their usual places, Cup with red wine. Also on Altar are Tarot Atu XV, the Devil, a consecrated Kamea of Saturn, a ball point pen of black ink, pine cones, evergreen twigs or branches, sprigs of ivy. Chair in southwest, facing northeast. Ritual Book on stand by chair. Incense is a mixture of frankincense, pine needles and bay leaves, with a drop or two of musk oil and/or honey and/or turpentine and/or semen and/or blood.

After bathing prior to the Rite, anoint throat, wrists, genitals, and feet with natural or synthetic oil of musk. Sky-clad or robed, girded and sandaled, enter Temple, salute Altar, circumambulate from west to north to east to south, light lamp of Secret Flame, ignite charcoal, take lighter or matches to west to northeast, light candles, go to east to south, return lighter or matches, go to southwest, sit. Pause. Then read aloud:

I am sitting in Yesod, in the Sphere of Levannah the Moon, looking upon Path Thirty that leads from Yesod to Hod. According to the Sepher Yetzirah, "the Thirtieth Path is the Exciting Intelligence because thence is created the spirit of every creature under the supreme Orb, and the assemblage of them all." To Path Thirty is assigned the zodiacal sign of Capricorn the Goat, the Hebrew letter QOPH which means Back of the Head and Tarot Atu XV, the Devil.

Stand. Go to north to east to south. Cast incense upon the coals in the Thurible and cense Altar, saying:

> [Censing left] *Eko, Eko, Azarak!*
> [Censing right] *Eko, Eko, Zomelak!*
> [Censing forward] *Eko, Eko, Kernunnos!*

Replace Thurible. Go to southwest, face Altar, take Tarot card, hold it high and say:

Lord of the Gates of Matter! Child of the Forces of Time! Khem! Set! Priapus! Pan!

> *Hear me, Lord of the Stars!*
> *For thee have I worshipped ever-*
> *With stains and sorrows and scars,*
> *With joyful, joyful Endeavor.*
> *Hear me, O lilywhite goat,*
> *Crisp as a thicket of thorns,*
> *With a collar of gold for thy throat,*
> *A scarlet bow for thy horns.*

Thou art the Generative Power! Thou art the Creative Force! [Lower card, stare at it for a moment.] *The Sign of Capricorn is rough, harsh, dark, even blind, the impulse to create takes no account of reason, custom or foresight. It is divinely unscrupulous, sublimely careless of result.* [Pause.] *O Man-Goat of Mendes, I hear your words—"Thou hast no right but to do thy will. Do that, and no other shall say nay.*

For pure will, unassuaged of purpose, delivered from the lust of result, is in every way perfect."—I hear and I obey.

Replace card. Touch Kamea of Saturn and say:

Old One of the Night of Time! Kronos! Saturn! Your Sphere is Shabbathai for you are the Old Lord of the Sabbath! May I truly observe and celebrate the Sabbath. Mark me with your sign! [Take pen in right hand and make symbol of Saturn on left palm, replace pen, fold middle and ring fingers of left hand to hide the symbol, holding them with thumb, extend forefinger and little finger.] It is not I that make this sign, it is Zazel, the Spirit of Saturn, that makes it. [Raise left arm high.] The Sign of the Old One! In it is power! [Lower arm.]

Now look at and genuflect to the Secret Flame on the center of the Altar. Say:

The Secret Flame burns in the Stones of Adam Kadmon, powering the Machinery of the Universe. [Take the stones or nuts, warm them at the flame and apply to back of skull and nape of neck and to private parts.] May my instincts be sharpened! May my creative force by strengthened! Vesta, Vesta, be strong in me, and as I will, so mote it be! [Replace stones or nuts on Altar.]

Dance deosil around Altar singing a song of aspiration such as "The Impossible Dream" or "Climb Every Mountain." Let leaping or jumping be included in the dance, imitating the fondness of the goat for high places. Finish dance in southwest. Face Altar and say:

I have climbed the high place! I shall ever seek the high places for they are home to me as my true race is of the starry skies. Yet I despise not the low places, nor the places in between. All places and all things are habitations and expressions of the One who is the All, the All who is the One! Therefore I shall continue searching to find, to have and to hold, complete appreciation of all existing things.

The Vice of this Path is Deceitfulness. Henceforth I abhor and forswear all deceit! The Virtue of this Path is Diplomacy. I shall try to be diplomatic in all my relationships with all forms of life everywhere. To this end I drink. [Drink the wine in the Cup.] Such is my will, and so mote it be.

Sit. Enter the Silence. Perform Closing Exercises of Temple Rite.

The Victory Wreath

Prerequisite: Rite of the Thirtieth Path.

Time: Waxing Moon in Aries. If possible on a Tuesday.

Black Pillar in northeast corner of room, White Pillar in southeast corner. Before White Pillar is a stand, facing northwest, with statue or picture of Venus or Tarot Atu III, the Empress, flanked by green candles, and, if desired, a Victory Wreath of laurel leaves. Altar in center of room, so placed its eastern side faces the southeast. On Altar is a tall red candle in holder, Tarot Atu IV, the Emperor, consecrated Kameas of Mars and the Sun, and the four Magical Instruments in their usual places, Cup with red wine. Scattered over Altar or formed in a wreath around base of candle or in low vases is a profusion of red flowers. Chair in northwest, facing southeast. By its side is stand with Ritual Book. Incense: dragon's blood if possible, otherwise frankincense.

Robed, girded and sandaled, enter and perform Opening Exercises of Temple Rite as given in Rite of Path Thirty-One [from entering Temple to Sign of the Enterer]. Go deosil to ignite charcoal and light candles. Proceed to west, sit. Read aloud:

Following the Path of the Serpent, I am in Yesod facing Path Twenty-Eight which leads from Yesod to Netzach. According to the Sepher Yetzirah the Twenty-Eighth Path is "the Intelligence of Will and is so called because it is the means of preparation of all and each created being, and by this Intelligence the existence of the Primordial Wisdom becomes known." To Path Twenty-Eight is assigned the zodical sign of Aries, the Ram, the Hebrew letter LAMED which means Ox Goad, and Tarot Atu IV, the Emperor. The theme and aim of this Path is Action, but action that is wisely directed to the end of attaining Power, Authority, Leadership. Henceforth, I want no action that is without purpose. I will myself to never forget this.

Stand, circumambulate to south, put incense in Thurible and cense Altar, saying:

> [to the left] *Ave (Ah-vay) Mars, Ruler of Aries!*
> [to the right] *Ave Sol, Great Sun, exalted therein!*
> [forward] *Ave Michael, Archangel of Fire!*

Replace Thurible, go to southwest, face Altar, take Tarot card and hold it high, saying:

Son of the Morning! Chief among the Mighty! Self-confident you are, frank, courageous and independent.[Lower card and gaze at it for a moment.] *In Alchemy this card represents Sulphur, the male fiery energy of the Universe. In the Hindu teachings this is Rajas, the swift creative energy, the initiative of all being. The power of the Emperor is a generalization of the paternal power. He bears a sceptre and an orb surmounted by a Maltese Cross, signifying that his energy has reached a successful issue, that his government has been established. May it be so with* [here name those potential "fathers—whether of a child, a cause, an organization or a government—for whom you wish success] *and with me.* [Again hold the card high, then replace it on Altar.]

Touch Kamea of Mars and say:

Mighty Mars, ruler of Aries! Horus, Crowned and Conquering! Militant you are, energetic, enthusiastic and impulsive. Share your power with [here repeat names as above] *and with me, as you did in generous measure with Alexander the Great, Julius Caesar, Richard the Lion-Hearted, Napoleon Bonaparte and many another.*

Touch Kamea of the Sun and say:

Exalted is Sol, the Sun, Father and King of the Solar System, Solar Logos! Word of the Father! Holy Avatar of God! God made manifest in human form! Osiris! Rama! Krishna! Orpheus! Mithras! Jesus the Christ! Gautama the Buddha! Exalted you are, exalted you will ever be! [Kneel.] *I worship thee and await thine again coming!* [Adore in silence for a moment, then rise.] *How may I serve and follow thee? How may I prepare for thy coming?* [Pause.] *Thus saith the Lord to me, "Set fire to thyself; thus shalt thou become a burning and a shining light." So be it, Lord. Thy word is law.* [Cup hands around candle flame.] *Burn, fire, burn! As you burn upon the Altar, burn thou in me!*

Dance, march or strut deosil around Altar, cadence-counting or shouting or singing a victory song, anything from your old school song to the Marine's Hymn. Finish dance in northwest, face Altar, take Cup and hold it high, saying:

Achieve every possibility! Find thyself in every Star! The essence of this Rite is the urge that impels a new cycle with new ideas, new plans, new thoughts, new proposals—leading to victory. [Extend Cup toward Netzach.] *To Victory!* [Drink, Replace Cup] *The Virtue of this Path is Determination. May this virtue ever be mine! The Vices of this Path are officiousness, egotism, rashness. I avoid them like the plague. The Magic Powers of this Path are the Ability to Rule and the Power of Consecrating. To the one I aspire; I have already expressed the other.* [Take Wand and hold it high.] *I have said what I have said. By the power of Yah, the Yod of Tetragrammaton, and the Wand of Will, so mote it be.*

Replace Wand. Sit. Enter the Silence. Perform Closing Exercises of Temple Rite.

The Crossroad

Required Reading: *New Model of the Universe* by P.D. Ouspensky.

Prerequisite: The Rite of Path Twenty-Eight.

Time: Waning Moon in Sagittarius. If possible, on a Friday.

The "Veil of Paroketh" reaches completely across the eastern wall. This may be ceiling-to-floor drapes entirely covering the wall with an opening in the center, it may be tokened with ordinary gauze-type window curtains hung at the center of the wall, or it may simply be visualized, the Crucifix may be on a stand against center of eastern is a Crucifix, a cross with a corpus, in center of wall. In case the Veil is visualized and Crucifix may be on a stand against center of eastern wall and covered with a veil or a handkerchief, or the Crucifix may be fastened to the eastern wall and veiled. Against center of southern wall is a stand with a statue or picture of Venus or Tarot Atu III, the Empress, with green candles. Beside it to the east is the white Pillar and to the west the stand with censing equipment. Against center of northern wall is a stand with statue or picture of Mercury or Tarot Atu I, the Magician, with lavender candles. Beside it to the east is the black Pillar. On Altar in center of room are a bouquet of yellow (or orange) and purple flowers (iris, if possible), four tall white candles in holders at the four corners, a book of matches at northeast corner, and the four Magical Instruments in their proper places, Cup with water. Also on Altar are Tarot Atu XIV, Temperance, Tarot Atu XIX, the Sun, consecrated Kameas of Jupiter and the Sun, a nail, a bow and arrow which may be a child's toy or even a picture since the use is symbolic, and two brandy glasses, snifters or stemmed goblets, one of which contains a small amount of brandy. Chair in west, facing east. By it is stand with Ritual Book. Incense: a mixture of equal parts of frankincense and myrrh.

Robed, girded and sandaled, enter Temple, salute Altar, circumambulate deosil lighting candles in north and on northwest and northeast of Altar, candles in south and on southeast and southwest of Altar, igniting charcoal, then returning to west. Sit. Pause. Read aloud:

I am in Yesod. Before me is a crossroad. From Hod in the north on my left to Netzach in the south on my right is Path Twenty-Seven. Directly before me, leading from Yesod to Tiphareth (Tif-FAR-eth) is Path Twenty-Five. The Paths cross in the center of the Temple where stands the Altar. A crossroad! The witches, or rather the Wicca, the wise ones, used to sometimes meet at a crossroad, a place where roads cross. Esoteric tradition affirms that when the pupil is ready, the master appears. It further affirms that the Inductor into the mysteries, the Hierophant, the Wise One, the Teacher, the Mother of Wisdom, is met at a crossroad, where roads cross. This Rite I am now performing signifies such a meeting and its performance sets the imponderable forces at work to bring about such a meeting. Now I can start looking for the Stranger Who Can Show the Way at crossroads, anywhere from the crossing of two dusty lanes far out in the country to the intersection of Forty-Second Street and Broadway in New York or Hollywood and Vine in Los Angeles. But why does it have to be a stranger? Perhaps it is someone I already know. I rather think that the crossroads refer to a climax or time of choice of direction in one's life. Am I at a crossroads in my life? [Pause to consider.] Is this a time of change of direction for me? Is there now a climax in my life? Are there choices of direction new before me? [Pause to consider.] Perhaps. So I am to meet someone who can show me the way to Magical Attainment! That would be wonderful and most welcome. I wonder who it could be? It could be a person, even someone I already know. It could be a discarnate human being, even a non-human astral entity. Or perhaps it is my own Holy Guardian Angel, mine own Higher Self, my Oversoul, the I AM THAT I AM part of me, the Everlasting Child of God Self. May it be so! May it be so! [Pause. Stand.] I am on Path Twenty-Five. The Twenty-Fifth Path is "the Administrative Intelligence because it directs all the operations of the Planets and concurs therein." To this Path is assigned Sol, the Sun, the Hebrew letter BETH, which means House, and Tarot Atu XIX, the Sun. On the Noble Eightfold Path this is Right Rapture. The Virtue is Rulership. But before one can rule that which is without one must first learn to rule that which is within. I aspire to complete self-control. The Sin of this Path is Pride. I need to exercise control to keep a healthy self-esteem from inflating into the Sin of Pride. The Vice of this Path is Dictativeness. I'm ashamed to admit that sometimes I can be plain bossy. I must watch this.

Go deosil to south, put incense in Thurible, cense Altar, return Thurible. Go to west, face Altar, take Tarot Atu XIX, the Sun. Hold it high and say:

Lord of the Fire of the World! Reveal to me your Mystery! [Lower card and gaze at it for a moment.] This card represents Solar Energy. We know that all the energy we have on earth comes to us from the Sun. The masters say, "In the Sun is the Secret of the Spirit." [Pause to contemplate.] The secret of the spirit is—energy? The card depicts children—young human life—beginning of self-consciousness. The secret of the spirit is self-conscious energy! [Say it several times wonderingly.] God is Self-Conscious Energy! [Then shout it triumphantly.] God is Self-Conscious Energy! [Carrying the card, dance joyfully deosil around Altar. Return to west, re-examine the card.] Master Therion says that Atu XIX shows the Twins shining forth and playing. The twins are the Vau and final He of Tetragrammaton. Yod (yode) is Chokmah (hoke-muh), the first He (hay) is Binah (BEE-nah), Vau (vahv) is Zoar Anpin (ZOE-ahr AHN-pin) which is Tiphareth (Tuh-FAR-eth) with Chesed (HAY-sed), Geburah (hard q, quh-BOO-ruh), Netzach, Hod and Yesod as appendages, final He is Malkuth. Zoar Anpin is the Bridegroom. His bride is Malkuth. The Kingdom. The book 777 lists Atu XIX as representing the fighting of Horus and Set. Now Horus is Light, Set is Darkness. Here we have boy and girl, bridegroom and bride, light and darkness. This Path goes between the light and dark Pillars, the opposite principles. Opposite principles are such as male and female, light and dark, up and down, summer *and winter, even good and evil. The fighting, the playing, of opposite principles. What does all this mean?* [Replace card on Altar. Pause in wonderment. Then speak in a tone and manner as you think a great Oracle of ancient times would do:]

> *Myriad are the pairs of opposites;*
> *The opposing principles contend not,*
> *Rather do they co-habit and co-operate*
> *To produce the phenomena of the universe,*
> *For without them the universe would not be;*
> *This is the Dual Manifestation of Truth,*
> *Realization of it brings Right Rapture.*

Pause in deep contemplation of what has been said. Touch Kamea of the Sun and say:

Sol, Great Sun! Seat and symbol of the Cosmic Christ, the Cosmic Buddha! Thou Single Source of Light and Life whose scattered seeds we are on earth! Praise be unto thee! I hear your words: "Give forth thy light to all without doubt, the clouds and shadows are no matter for thee. Make Speech and Silence, Energy and Stillness, twin forms of thy play." I hear and I obey.

Take the nail from the Altar and stare at it for a moment. Then say:

The Hebrew letter Vau is associated with the Sephirah (suh-fear-uh) Tiphareth. Vau means nail. In Hebrew Vau is used as a connective, like we use the word "and." A nail is a fastener, it joins or binds. It connects things. Of course it is also a Dagger, a Sword and a Rod or Wand, hence is masculine, positve, airy, fiery. Evidently it is of use in traversing this Path. [Tuck nail under girdle.]

Go from west to north to east. Face eastern wall. Vividly visualize the Veil of Paroketh before you. Say:

The Veil of Paroketh is before me. I cannot see beyond it. It hinders my further progress on this Path. Beyond is Tiphareth, the Sphere of the Sun and the Seat of Christ Consciousness, of Buddhic Consciousness. But the glory of that is veiled to me. A veil! The Veil of the Temple of Jerusalem was rent from top to bottom at the time of the Crucifixion. Isis stands naked in the East in her mystery School Temple, her beauty is veiled to the eyes of the profane. When a man looks upon her naked beauty he dies, for she takes him, he is joined to her, he is born anew, he becomes one with her. Christ suffers his passion nailed to the cross. "Unless a man die and be born again he can in no wise enter the Kingdom of Heaven." A rebirth is a transmutation. I seek transmutation, a spiritual rebirth, becoming born again in order to penetrate the veil and attain Tiphareth Consciousness. When I attain that I will have reached Adeptship, Mastery. But the Veil of Paroketh presently bars me. I shall return to this place again! I shall return! Now let me explore the other Path.

Replace nail on Altar. Go deosil to north, face south. Say:

I am now on Path Twenty-Seven that leads from Hod to Netzach. The Twenty-seventh Path is "called the Renewing Intelligence because the Holy God renews by it all the changing things which are part of this creation of worlds." It is the Path of Nature's Re-Cycling. To it is assigned the zodiacal sign of Sagittarius, the Archer or the Centaur, the Hebrew letter SAMECH which means Prop, and Tarot Atu XIV, Temperance.

Go to Altar, Take Tarot Atu XIV, hold it high and say:

Daughter of the Reconcilers! Bringer Forth of New Life! Reveal to me your Mystery! [Lower card and gaze at it for a moment.] *In your hands you hold two vases, emptying the contents of one into the other. When you have done so you reverse the process, pouring back and forth, emptying each in turn into the other. Why do you do this? What does it mean? On you breast is a square enclosing an upright equilateral triangle—the magic sign of the Tarot. One of your feet is on dry land, the other in water. On your forehead is the symbol of the Sun. The glory of a golden crown shines on a high mountain in the far distance behind you, a path leads thereto but its course is lost in hilly terrain. Yellow Iris blooms where you are standing.* [Pause.] *This is the Mystery of the Fourth Dimension, the Mystery of Time. We think of time as flowing in one direction only, from the past to the present to the future. This is because the consicous mind is so structured as thus to perceive time. But in reality time flows in different directions and is not necessarily always linear in nature.* [Pause.] *In tarot divination this card signifies promotion if dignified or upright and demotion if ill-dignified or upside down. Sagittarius is the Centaur, half animal, half human. The path shown in this card is the same path shown in the Waning Moon card, the path of evolution. Temperance, the Daughter of the Reconcilers, tells me evolution is not always necessarily forward, upward, for the better. The Centaur shows the animal transmuted by aspiration into the human. The Werewolf, on the other hand, shows the human transmuted by blood-lust into the animal. All this is associated with the Fourth Dimension. [Pause.] The secret of this Path then is Transmutation.*

Replace card. Touch Kamea of Jupiter and say:

Mighty Jupiter! Jove! Ruler of Sagittarius! All-Father in three forms of Fire, Air, Water! Generous Giver of Gifts! Greater Benefic! The Magical Power I pray for is Transmutation. Base metal to gold, animal to human, human to divine! Hear my prayer addressed to thee, and as my will, so mote it be! I hear thy words—"Perfection presides over Transmutation. Self-sacrifice and self-control govern the wheel. Transmute all wholly into the images of thy will, bringing each to its true token of perfection."—I hear, I seek to understand that I may obey.

Touch bow and arrow and say:

Diana Huntress! Bringer Forth of Life! The Bow and Arrow are yours. They are assigned to this Rite. Go thou before me in the hunt.

Remove Girdle, robe and sandals. Crouch, emulating the babe in the womb. Then be born as a primitive form of life, slithering along floor deosil around Altar. Then be a frog, a bird, a raccoon, a wild cat, a hoofed animal, an ape, hissing, croaking, whistling, grunting, making animal sounds, imitating animal movement. Several times around Altar. Then stand upright as a human, finish dance in the west. Reclothe. Say:

First the stone, then the plant, then the animal, then the human! So have I transmuted. I seek further transmutation.

Take the glass with brandy in right hand, the empty glass in left hand. Pour brandy from right to left, then reverse the process saying:

Pour thine own freely from the vase in thy right hand and lose no drop. Hath not thy left hand a vase?

Drink the brandy. Replace glasses. Take cup and offer it, saying:

The Virtue of this Path is Directness. Direct may I ever be. [Offer Cup to the east.] *I shall return! The Vice of this Path is Wastefulness. Wasteful may I never be!* [Drink water in Cup, replace Cup on Altar, sit.] *I see a rainbow arching across from Hod to Netzach!* [Vividly visualize.] *The Path of the Arrow goes straight up the Tree of Life on the Pillar of Mildness. The Bow of Promise is before me.* [Look to the east.] *I shall return!*

Enter the Silence. Perform Closing Exercises of Temple Rite.

The Path of the Messenger

Preliminary: Since in ascending the Tree of Life Path Twenty-Six is the intellectual approach to Spiritual Consciousness, the Seeker is urged to sharpen, widen, deepen and heighten his intellect by a program of systematic study of the social, physical and biological sciences, especially those in which he is uninformed. And an acquaintance with a language other than his own native tongue should be acquired. A journey to a foreign country is also most appropriate at this time. If this is impossible, then visits should be made to places or neighborhoods where the way of life is "foreign" or at least different to one's own.

Required reading: *The Kybalion* by Three Initiates. *The Hero with a Thousand Faces* by Joseph Campbell. *The Occult, a History* by Colin Wilson. *Occult Psychology* by Alta La Dage.

Time: Waxing Moon on a Wednesday early in the morning, mid-afternoon or late evening.

On Altar are Tarot Atu I, the Magician, a consecrated Kamea of Mercury, the four Magical Instruments in their proper places, Cup with red wine, and a ribbon-tied rolled sheet of parchment or paper on which has been copied:

THE EMERALD TABLET OF HERMES

True, without falsehood, certain and to be depended upon, that which is above is as that which is below, and that which is below is as that which is above, for the performance of the miracles of the One Thing. As all things owe their existence to the Only One, so all things have their birth from this One Only Thing, the most hidden. The Sun is its father, the Moon its mother, the Wind carries it in its belly, its nurse is the Earth. This One Only Thing is the father of all things in the universe, the father of all perfection. Thou shalt separate the earth from the fire, the subtle from the gross, suavely, and with great ingenuity. It ascends from earth to heaven and descends again to earth, and receives the power of the superiors and of the inferiors. So hast thou the glory of the whole world; therefore, let all obscurity flee before thee. This is the strong force of all forces, overcoming every subtle and penetrating every solid thing. So the world was created. Hence were all wonderful adaptations, of which this is the manner. The arrangements to follow this road are hidden. For this reason I am called Hermes Trismegistus, one in essence, but three in aspect. In this trinity is hidden the wisdom of the whole world. It is ended now, what I have said concerning the operation of the Sun. Finish of the Tabula Smaragdina.

Two or four tall lavender-colored candles and flowers appropriate to Mercury such as violets or lilac or lavender-colored artificial flowers may also be on Altar if desired.

The Pillars are about two feet apart against center of eastern wall, black pillar north, white south. Between them is stand with crucifix or statue or picture of Christ or Buddha with white candles on either side. Stand with Ritual Book by chair in west. Incense: lavender, mace, mastic or storax.

Perform Opening Exercises of Temple Rite, censing the Altar after the Sign of the Enterer. Seated in the west, read aloud:

The Twenty-sixth Path of the Tree of Life is "the Serving Intelligence and is so called because it is the means whereby the Sun of Righteousness illuminates the mind of man and delivers the message of Tiphareth." To it is assigned the Hebrew letter PE which means

Mouth. Also assigned here is Tarot Atu I, the Magician, the Juggler with the Secret of the Universe, whose astrological equivalent is the planet Mercury. This Path echoes what the Three Initiates affirm in The Kybalion that "the All is Mind; the Universe is Mental."

The virtue of this Path is Truthfulness. What is truth? The conformity of cognition to reality. Ever I seek to know the truth and truthful may I ever be. The Sin of this Path is Envy. Envious may I never be. The Vices of this Path are Falsehood and Dishonesty. The great ones of this Path have in times past been accused of these vices. Were they all liars and cheats? I cannot believe so. Perhaps their cognition of reality differed from that of their accusers. Perhaps they were marching to the beat of a different drum. Perhaps some believed the end justified the means. I must observe and analyze any tendencies in myself toward falsehood and dishonesty. Even if others should construe my affirmation of the reality of Magic and my effort to practice Magic as false and dishonest, I intend to be truthful and honest both to myself and others.

Path Twenty-Six is the Path of the Messenger and many named is he—Thoth, Tahuti, Hermes, Enoch, Mercury, Herne and many another. Master of all arts and sciences, perfect in all crafts. Ruler of Three Worlds, Scribe of the Gods and Keeper of the Books of Life, Thoth Hermes Trismegistus—The Three Times Greatest, the "First Intelligence"—is regarded as the embodiment of the Universal Mind. Among the arts and sciences which is affirmed Hermes revealed to mankind were medicine, chemistry, law, art, astrology, music, rhetoric, magic, philosophy, geography, mathematics, geometry, anatomy and oratory. As Thoth or Tahuti we first find him in the mythology of Egypt. It was Hermes who was known to the Jews as Enoch, called the "Second Messenger of God." He is Hermes in the mythology of the Greeks, who later became the Mercury of the Latins. He is revered through the form of the planet Mercury because its body is nearest the Sun, seat and symbol of the Solor Logos.

Stand, say:

> Lord Hermes, Messenger of Light!
> Thee I invoke with all my might!
> Messenger whose messenger I would be-
> Thee I invoke, come thou unto me!
> [Circumambulate deosil while saying:]

> *Lord Hermes, come to me!*
> *Lord Hermes, come to me!*
> *Messenger whose messenger I would be—*
> *Thee I invoke, come thou unto me!*

Return to west, face Altar, take Tarot I, the Magician, hold it high and say:

Magus of Power! Juggler with the Secret of the Universe! Bearer of the Wand! Messenger of the Gods bearing the Word of Creation whose speech is Silence! Reveal to me your Mystery! [Lower card, gaze at it for a moment.] *This card represents continuous creation. Hermes not only bears the Word, he is the Word: "In the beginning was the Word, and the Word was with God, and the Word was God. All things were made by him, and without him was not anything made that was made."* [Pause in comtemplation.]

Replace card. Touch each instrument while saying:

> *With the Wand createth he.*
> *With the Cup preserveth he.*
> *With the Dagger destroyeth he.*
> *With the Coin redeemeth he.*

Re-study the card. Take Wand and make a figure eight over head. Then say:

The symbols of Atu I, the Magician, all refer to powers of the self-conscious phase of personal mental activity. These powers are directed primarily to the control of forces and things below the self-conscious level. The energy utilized comes from above, from superconsciousness, from Tiphareth. It is fixed and modified by acts of attention. Concentration is the great secret of the magical art. True concentration allows the personality to become a free, unobstructed channel for the passage downward and outward of superconscious radiant energy expressing the will and the wisdom of the Higher Self. Herein is the secret of all true volition. All magic is in the will.

Assume the stance of the Magician and say:

"Will! Know! Dare! and be Silent! The true Self is the meaning of the true Will: Know thy Self through thy Way. Calculate well the formula of thy way. Create freely; absorb joyously; divide intently; consolidate completely. Work thou, omnipotent, omniscient, omnipresent, in and for Eternity."

Replace Wand. Take up Kamea of Mercury, and say:

> *Lord Hermes, come to me!*
> *Lord Hermes, come to me!* -
> *Messenger whose messenger I would be—*
> *Thee I invoke, come thou unto me!*
>
> *Thou puttest the babe into woman's womb,*
> *Thou leadest the dead from the dreary tomb;*
> *Thy muses hymn thy holy name;*
> *Thine aid is sought in gymnastic game.*
>
> *Measureless thy store of wealth!*
> *Limitless thy core of health!*
> *Knowledge of truth is thine to give,*
> *Thy way of life is the life to live.*
>
> *Thou givest ability to communicate*
> *Without the need to prevaricate.*
> *Science and language are thine to share*
> *with them that follow thy precepts fair.*
>
> *Thine serpent-twined Caduceus,*
> *Thine incantations effectuous*
> *Produce health and balance wise*
> *Upon the earth and in the skies.*

Replace kamea. Take Cup, offer it and say:

> *Lord Hermes, thou of many a name,*
> *Whose good is, was, will be the same;*
> *Whose oracles speak of what will be—*
> *To thee I drink! Come thou unto me!*

Drink. Replace Cup. Say:

The Pentagram, the five-pointed star, expresses the spirit's domination over the elements, and it is by this sign that we bind the Sylphs of Air, the Salamanders of Fire, the Undines of Water and the Gnomes of Earth. It is the star of the Magi, the burning star of the Gnostic schools, the sign of intellectual superiority. It is the symbol of the Word made Flesh. The Sign of the Pentagram is called also the Sign of the Microcosm. Its complete comprehension is the key that admits into Tiphareth.

Go east, face the Pillars and perform the Lesser Ritual of the Pentagram.

LESSER RITUAL OF THE PENTAGRAM

Facing East, perform the Qabalistic Cross. Right arm stretched straight before you, forefinger pointing, other fingers clasped to palm by thumb, draw a large five-pointed star in the air, visualizing the lines of the star as fire. Draw the Pentagram by connecting the periods of the diagram from one to six:

Say the Deity Name: *IHVH* (Spell it Yod, He, Vau, He, or pronounce it Yahweh).

Turn right to south, draw the star in fire, say the Deity Name: *ADNI* (Adonai, ah-doh-NOE-ee).

Turn right to west, draw the star in fire, say the Deity Name: *AHIH* (Eheieh, ay-HEE-yuh).

Turn right to north, draw the star in fire, say the Diety Name: *AGLA* (AH-glah).

Turn right to face east again. Extending the arms on either side so as to make your body a cross, say:

> *Before me Raphael; (rah-FAH-ell)*
> *Behind me Gabriel; (GAH-bree-ell)*
> *On my right hand, Michael; (MICK-ah-ell)*
> *On my left hand, Auriel; (AH-ree-ell)*
> *For about me flames the Pentagram,*
> *And in the column stands the six-rayed Star.*

Repeat the Qabalistic Cross. Long pause. Then face Altar and say:

> Lord Hermes, come to me!
> Lord Hermes, come to me!
> Messenger whose messenger I would be—
> Thee I invoke, come thou unto me!

Kneel. Vividly visualize in the east a luminous haze distributing itself throughout the atmosphere until the air becomes a mass of shining particles. See the particles coalesce into a larger-than-life form—that of Hermes. The body seems partly transparent so that the heart and brain can be seen pulsating and radiant. Then see the heart change into a long-billed and long-legged wading bird like a heron, an ibis, and the brain into a flashing emerald. In Hermes' right hand is a winged rod entwined with serpents. See him in a blaze of glory which fades into nothingness. Before the vision is gone say:

> All hail to thee, Thoth Hermes, Thrice Greatest!
> All hail to thee, Prince of Men!

Get to feet. Take parchment or paper roll from Altar and, carrying it, circumambulate deosil. Return to west, sit, unroll and silently read the Emerald Tablet. Enter the Silence. Then return the tablet to the Altar and perform Closing Exercises of Temple Rite.

The Queen's Gate

Preliminary: Path Twenty-Four on the Tree of Life is the aesthetic and emotional approach to Spiritual Consciousness. Therefore the Theurgist should seek expansion of the aesthetic and emotional aspects of his nature by considerable experience in at least three (if possible, all) of the following:

1. Conjugal love and family life. The life of a loving couple who are having and raising children.

2. The Arts. If any talent, then training and expression of ability in painting, sculpture, architecture, photography, music, voice, dance, drama. If talent or training is lacking, then cultivation of appreciation of the arts, through collection of art objects or recordings or reproductions, visits to art museums, attendance at concerts, opera, ballet, theatre.

3. Poetry and romantic literature. Familiarity with the poems and novels of the great English and American poets and romantic novelists. Cultivation of interest in contemporary poetry. Attempt at some creative writing of one's own.

4. Nature. A life lived close to nature. At the least, long leisurely visits or vacations spent at the seashore, a lake, a national or state park, or in a setting where nature is particularly lovely.

Time: Waxing Moon on a Friday, early in the morning, midafternoon or late evening.

On Altar are Tarot Atu III, the Empress, a consecrated Kamea of Venus, the four Magical Instruments in their proper places, Cup with Rose wine, green or pink candles and a profusion of sweet-smelling flowers. Pillars against middle of eastern wall with stand between them, on stand is crucifix or statue or picture of Christ or Buddha with white candles. Ritual Book on stand by chair in west. Incense: sandalwood.

Perform Opening Exercises of Temple Rite, censing the Altar after the Sign of the Enterer. (If possible, have records or tapes of your favorite love songs playing softly during the following.) Seated in west, read aloud:

The Twenty-Fourth Path of the Tree of Life connects Netzach and Tiphareth. It is "the Imaginative Intelligence and is so called because it gives a likeness to all the similitudes which are created in like manner similar to its harmonious elegancies." To this Path is assigned the letter DALETH, which means Door, the planet Venus and Tarot Atu III, The Empress.

The title of Atu III is the Empress and means literally "she who sets in order." She is the feminine ruling power, the consort of the Emperor, Atu IV. Her name contrasts with High Priestess which indicates the cold virginity of a cloistered devotee of the gods. In like manner, mythology contrasts the warm love goddess Venus with Diana the virgin goddess of the Moon. Actually there is no fundamental difference between the High Priestess and the Empress; but the High Priestess symbolizes the virgin state of the cosmic subconsciousness as it is in itself, whereas the Empress typifies the productive, generating activities of the same subconsciousness after it has been impregnated by seed-ideas originating at the subconscious level represented by the Magician.

Pause in contemplation of what has been read. Then stand, go to Altar, take Tarot Atu III and hold it high, saying:

Daughter of the Mighty Ones! Great Empress! Great thou art and greatly to be honored! I honor thee! Honor thou me by revealing to me thy Mystery!

Lower card to eye level. Gaze at it for a moment. Then say:

This is the Door or Gate of the Equilibrium of the Universe. Her yellow hair is bound by a green laurel wreath, that of Netzach, and her hair symbolizes radiant energy. She is surrounded by luxuriant plant growth—the idea here conveyed is that the growth and organization of the plant-world is the work of cosmic energy operating at subconsious levels. Thus people who know how to reach the consciousness of plants can do almost anything with them. Hers is the secret, she is the secret, and she is Love! The empress wears a crown of twelve stars and has a crescent moon under her feet. The stars are six-pointed, or hexagrams, to show that she has dominion over the laws of the Macrocosm, or great world. The crown of twelve stars also symbolizes the Zodiac, the year, and time. The silver lunar crescent under the Empress' feet indicates the fact that the subconscious activities she symbolizes have their basis in the primary powers of subconsciousness which the Tarot pictures in the High Priestess. Psychologically, the Empress represents subconsciousness as the mother of ideas, the generatrix of mental images, hence this her Path is called "the Imaginative Intelligence." What says she to me?

Again elevate the card and say:

"Love and let love! Rejoice in every shape of love, and get thy rapture and thy nourishment thereof! This is the harmony of the universe, that love unites the will to create with the understanding of that creation, understand thou thine own will! Beauty, display thine empire! Truth above thought's reach; the wholeness of the world is love!" I hear thy words, Mighty Queen, and I rejoice in them!

Replace card on Altar. Touch Kamea of Venus and say:

Goddess of Love! Hathor! Aphrodite! Venus! Lalita! Freya! Lady of Delight! Graciousness thou art, let me gracious be! Charmful thou art, let me charming be! Ask me not to leave thee, nor to return from following after thee; for whither thou goest I will go, where thou lodgest I will lodge, thy people shall be my people, and thy God my

God. [Tuck kamea under Girdle.] *The Girdle is your Magical Weapon. It was the first of mine. Henceforth, thou art mine and I am thine!*

Circumambulate deosil while saying:

> *Heav'nly, illustrious, laughter-loving queen,*
> *Seaborn, night-loving, of a gracious mien,*
> *Whate'er the heav'ns, encircling all, contain,*
> *Earth fruit producing, and the stormy main,*
> *Thy sway confesses, and obeys thy nod,*
> *Lovely attendant of the Brumal God.*
> *Goddess of marriage, charming to the sight,*
> *Mother of Loves, whom banquetings delight;*
> *Source of persuasion, secret, fav'ring queen,*
> *Illustrious born, apparent and unseen,*
> *Spousal, lupercal, and to men inclin'd,*
> *Prolific, most-desired, life-giving, kind.*
> *Come, Cyprus-born, be to my prayer inclin'd.*
> *For thee I call, with holy, reverent mind.*

Either turn up the volume of the music being played or begin singing your favority love-song or other appropriate song such as "Because" or "I Love You Truly." Dance several times deosil around Altar, happily, joyfully. Finish dance in the west, take Cup, offer it, saying:

Behold, thou art fair, my love; behold, thou art fair; thou hast dove's eyes. I am my beloved's, and beloved is mine.

Drink. Replace Cup. Sit. Enter the Silence. Perform Closing Exercises of Temple Rite.

The Way of the Twins

Preliminary: Develop and practice the ability to write legibly with the hand other than the one used naturally, or, develop and practice some manual skill requiring the use of both hands such as typing or playing piano or drums or feats of legerdemain or juggling. For a period of a few weeks at least, accept a job or task unrelated to your usual vocation, giving to it the required time, attention and energy to succeed in it but allowing it not to interfere with, disrupt or lessen your regular work. If a competent teacher is available, study and practice Hatha Yoga. Read at least two books on Astral Projection and begin experimenting with some of the techniques suggested therein.

Time: Waxing Moon in Gemini.

On Altar are Tarot Atu VI, the Lovers, a consecrated Kamea of Mercury and the four Magical Instruments in their proper places, Cup with water. Black Pillar behind chair in west. Beside chair is stand with Ritual Book. White Pillar in southwest corner of room. Incense: bay leaves, lavender. Robed, girded and sandaled, enter, salute Altar, go deosil to south, ignite charcoal, go to west, sit. Read aloud:

The Twenty-Third path of the Tree of Life is "called the House of Influence by the greatness of whose abundance the influx of good things upon created beings is increased and from the midst of the investigation the arcana and senses are drawn forth which dwell in its shade and which cling to it from the cause of all causes." Path Twenty-Three connects Hod and Geburah and is thus a part of the Pillar of Severity. To it is assigned the Hebrew letter AYIN which means Eye. Also assigned here is the Zodiacal Sign of Gemini the Twins, and Tarot Atu VI, the Lovers. The Virtue of this Path is Versatility. Versatile may I prove to be. Its Vice is Changeableness. Negatively changeable may I never be. Gemini is of the Airy Triplicity; it is Water of Air, as undulation or vibration, the bulk unmoved. It is a Mutable Sign, as liquid air. It is ruled by Mercury the Magician whom I claim as a sponsor and whom I love.

Stand. Go deosil to south, saying:

Thoth, Mercury, Hermes, Herne;
Thy love and aid I seek to earn.
As vassal and priest (priestess) accept thou me,
And as I pray, so mote it be!

Cast incense into Thurible and cense Altar, saying:

Evohe! Evohe! Thoth-Tahuti, Lord of Wisdom!
Evohe! Evohe! Hermes-Mercury, Lord of Magic!
Evohe! Evohe! Herne, Wicca-One, Lord of the Crossroads!

Replace Censer. Go Deosil to west. Take Tarot card, hold it high, and say:

Children of the Voice! Oracle of the Mighty Gods! Reveal to me your Mystery! [Lower card and gaze at it for a moment.] *This Tarot card is named the Lovers or the Twins or Temptation. Crowley says it properly should be called the Brothers. There are several versions of the card. In this one I see a green valley surrounded by distant hills. In the foreground are a woman and a man, nude. High above them is an Angel or Genie, winged and with outstretched arms, who, unseen, guides them. From a tree on which golden fruit is ripening a snake creeps down and whispers in the ear of the woman. The woman listens, smiling at first incredulously, then with curiosity. Then she speaks to the man and he also smiles and points with his hand to the valley all around them. A tree of flame-flowers is behind the man.*

Naturally this makes me think of Adam and Eve and their temptation in the Garden of Eden. Ouspensky says in explanation of this card, "The Wisdom which crawls on the ground said to Adam and Eve that they themselves knew what was good and what was evil. And they believed this because it was pleasant to think so. And then they ceased to hear the guiding voice. Equilibrium was destroyed. The enchanted world of Eden was closed to them. Everything appeared to them in a false light. And they became mortal. This Fall is the first sin of man and is perpetually repeated because man never ceases to believe in himself and his unaided ability to distinguish good and evil, and lives by this belief. Only when man has atoned this sin by great suffering can he pass out of the power of death and return to life." [Pause in contemplation.] *Another version of this card, that of Oswald Wirth, portrays a youth with a female figure on either side. One of these figures wears a golden crown and is winged, while the other is attired in flowing robes and on her head is a wreath of vine leaves. A winged Cupid above with bow and arrow is aiming his dart at the man, but in still another version the dart is aimed at the vine-crowned female.* [Pause to visualize.] *A fourth version of the card, possibly a corruption, shows a marriage ceremony in which a priest is uniting a youth and a maiden in wedlock, with a winged figure above transfixing the lovers with his dart.* [Pause to visualize.] *The occult key of this card is "Solve et coagula," dissolve and reform, which is Analysis and Synthesis. The first question, that of Analysis, is "Of what are things composed?" The second question, that of Synthesis, is "How shall we recombine them to our greater advantage?"* [Pause to reflect.] *In divination, when upright, this card means openness to inspiration, intuition, second sight, dexterity, versatility. When upside down it means instability, self-contradiction, triviality, indecision.* [Pause to memorize.] *For my advancement in Theurgy what says Atu VI to me?* [Again hold card high.] *"The Oracle of the Gods is the Child-Voice of Love in thine own Soul; hear thou it. Heed not the Siren-Voice of the Senses or the Phantom Voice of Reason; rest in Simplicity, and listen to the Silence." I hear and I obey.*

Replace card. Sit and enter the Silence. After a while, stand, touch Kamea of Mercury and say:

Mercury! As ruler of Gemini the Twins, you give dexterity and skill. Dexterous and skillful may I be!

Lift Kamea high and say:

On this the Eighteenth Path your Magical Powers are Prophecy and the Power of being in Two or more places at one time. I especially pray for the Power of Prophecy. May I thy prophet (prophetess) be! With Power of Prophecy endow thou me!

Kiss Kamea. With Kamea in right hand perform the Qabalistic Cross and the Sign of the Enterer. Then obey any impulse to speak, perhaps to prophesy. Or you may enter a state of partial or complete trance. Afterward replace Kamea and say:

Messenger whose message comes (now, not yet, dimly, clear) to me; thanks be to thee, thrice blessed be!

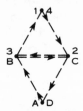

Take Dagger and with it make Hexagram of Air toward the east. Then draw symbol of Gemini as if within the Hexagram, saying:

Ararita! Gemini! Gemini! Gemini! Ararita!

Replace Dagger. Circumambulate deosil while saying:

I am walking the Path of the Twins. The twins are the Vau and He final of Tetragrammaton. I am each and both. My non-physical and physical are twins. My outer and my inner are twins. We walk together, "me and my shadow."

Stop in west. Take Cup, offer it, saying:

This Path connects Mercury and Mars. To them I drink. Hail, Brothers!

Drink. Replace Cup. Salute the Altar. Give Sign of Silence. The Rite is finished.

● ● ●

Note: In the Mysteries of Eleusis, Bay Leaves were used as incense to stimulate the power of prophecy.

Rite of Path Twenty-Two

Strong Right Arm of God

Preliminary: Acquire, exorcise and consecrate a Sword, a Scourge and a Chain. The sword may be especially made (if you can possibly make one yourself, by all means do so) with tempered steel blade straight, pointed, and sharp right up to the guard which is composed of two silver crescents back to back and between them are three spheres, one each of lead, tin and gold; the hilt is copper and the grip contains fixed quicksilver. Or a ceremonial sword may be purchased from a curio or antique shop or a Masonic supply house. You will probably have to make the scourge yourself even though they can sometimes be found in sex-oriented specialty shops. The Scourge is a whip with a wooden handle or shaft about two feet long and one-half to one inch in diameter, with three or more leather or rawhide thongs about two-and-a-half to three feet long tied or fastened to a notch on one end of the shaft. The loose ends of the thongs are knotted and the handle or shaft may be wrapped or bound with leather. The chain, from three to five feet in length, is such as a stainless steel dog leash. The consecration may simply be a Circled Cross or a more elaborate ceremony of your own devising.

Time: Waxing Moon on a Tuesday early in the morning, mid-afternoon or late evening.

On the Altar are the Sword, the Scourge, the Chain, Tarot Atu XVI, the Tower, a consecrated Kamea of Mars, the four Magical Instruments in their proper places, Cup with red wine in which has been put a drop of your own blood, two tall red candles and a profusion of bright red flowers. Black Pillar in northwest corner of room, White Pillar in southwest corner. Ritual Book on stand by chair in west. Censer with charcoal, lighter and container of incense on stand in south. Incense: dragon's blood if possible, otherwise frankincense. Records or tapes of band music. Robed, girded and sandaled, enter, salute Altar, go deosil lighting candles and charcoal, start music, go to west, sit. Read aloud:

Path Twenty-Two of the Tree of Life connects Geburah and Tiphareth. It is called "the Faithful Intelligence since because of it spiritual virtues are increased and all dwellers on earth are under its shadow." To it is assigned the Hebrew letter KAPH which means Fist, the planet Mars and Tarot Atu XVI, the Lightning-Struck Tower. Its Virtue is Strength. On the Noble Eightfold Path it is Right Energy. Its Sin is Anger. Its Vice is Harshness.

Stand. Say:

Elohim Gebor! (ell-oh-KEEM hard g ge-BORE) *Creative Omnipotent God! Your strong right arm is Mars, Krishna, Horus. Great is he, Lord of the Hosts of the Mighty, and greatly to be honored. I honor him.*

Go deosil to south. Take incense and cast it into thurible and cense Altar saying:

> *Evohe! Evohe! Mars!*
> *Evohe! Evohe! Krishna!*
> *Evohe! Evohe! Horus!*

Replace Censor. Go to west, face Altar, take Sword hold it high, point upward, and say:

Sword of Justice, Truth and Righteousness! All dwellers on earth are under your shadow! Whenever there is anything that has outlived its usefulness, you cut down and prune. Wherever there is selfishness, you impale. Wherever there is violence against the weak, you punish. Wherever there is the merciless use of strength, you counteract. Wherever there is sloth and dishonesty, you prod. And where there is removal of the landmarks set for our neighbor's protection, you restrain. Blessed are you and the arm that wields you!

Lower sword but still point upward as you say:

The upward pointing Sword is symbolic of great strength and success in works of justice, truth and righteousness. Its message is, "Dare, aspiring one! You will attain!" Invoked, it gives great power. [Elevate sword.] *In the Name of Elohim Gebor I invoke Din (deen), Justice, through Geburah, Strength, to visit* [here name those projects and people to whom you wish success] *and me.*

Slowly turn sword to point straight down and say:

But the downward pointing Sword is symbolic of great power and force in works of wrath and vengeance. Its message is, "How dare you, presumptuous fool! You will be punished!" Invoked, it brings great destruction. [Hold downward pointing sword in both hands, arms straight out in front.] *In the Name of Elohim Gebor I invoke Pachad* (PAKH-hahd), *Fear, through Geburah, Severity, to visit* [here name those projects which are inimical to general or particular welfare.] *"Vengeance is mine, I will repay!" saith the Lord.*

Pause. Return sword to Altar. Take Tarot card, hold it high and say:

Fortress of the Most High! Instrument of Karma! Reveal to me your Mystery! [Lower card and gaze at it for a moment.] *In divination when this card is upright it signifies quarrel, combat, danger, ruin, destruction of plans, even sudden death. To the gypsies it is a warning to strike camp, to move quickly so as to avoid danger.* [Reverse card.] *But oddly, when it is upside down it signifies escape from prison, escape from limitations. Thus it says to me:* [again lift card high] *"Break down the fortress of thine Individual Self, that thy Truth may spring free from the ruins."*

Lower card, pause in contemplation, return card to Altar. Touch Kamea of Mars and say:

Magnanimous, unconquer'd, boist'rous Mars, in darts rejoicing, and in bloody wars; Fierce and untam'd, whose mighty power can make the strongest walls from their foundations shake: Endow me, I pray you, of your vast power, great strength, unbounded energy! You delight in human blood, here's some of mine!

Take Cup, offer it, spill a little among the flowers, drink, replace Cup. Take up scourge and say:

The Scourge is yours. With it you punish. But also with it you drive. Drive me on in greater effort to use your gift of strength in order to achieve!

Remove robe and girdle. Whip yourself across the shoulders and back as you dance or march naked three times deosil around Altar. Returned to west, replace scourge on Altar, reclothe, kneel and say:

Thank you, Lord of the Hosts of the Mighty, for your lashes that drive me onward and upward.

Remain on knees for a moment or so, thinking of any unpleasant or painful circumstances in your life that perhaps instead of being punishment may well be goads to progress. Then stand, take chain and say:

But the chain restrains. I do not want to be restrained, I want to be free! Greater freedom to realize, to be and to become, is the very purpose of these Rites of the Path. Why, then, the Chain? What is to be restrained? [Pause.] *I must use the Right Energy and Strength of this Path to limit Anger and to restrain any tendencies toward Harshness and Cruelty.* [Hold chain high between upstretched hands.] *Constructive only may my anger be! May harshness have no place in me! May cruelty never be a part of me! This is my will, so mote it be!* [Pause. Then drape chain around neck and say:]

Chained am I to this physical body and this physical world. Chained am I to the workings of the Law of Karma. But I accept them not as limitations. I accept them as opportunities to experience so as to know! As such I wear the Chain proudly! [Strut Deosil once around Altar.]

Return to west, replace chain on Altar. Say:

To will, to know, to dare—to dare! To dare! To dare! I dare! [Place tip of right finger to closed lips.] *And to keep silent!*

Salute Altar. The Rite is finished.

The Way of the Alone One

Prerequisite: Knowlege of the influence of Virgo as a Sun Sign, Rising Sign, and occupying the Cusp of each House of the Horoscope.

Preliminary: The "Secret Flame" used in the Rite of Path Thirty is to be made portable so that it can be carried. Or any reasonable facsimile of the lamp carried by the Hermit in Tarot Atu IX is to be devised. At the least, a metal coffee-can with many holes punched into it, suspended by chains and containing a candle, will do. Also acquire a wooden staff such as a five to six foot pole.

Practice continence for at least seven days before the Rite. If at all possible spend three to seven days before the Rite completely alone. If this is quite impossible, then absolute minimum communication with others during the twenty-four hour period before the Rite. Fast during this period, taking only a little water.

Time: Waxing Moon in Virgo.

On the Altar is the Lamp of the Secret Flame, Tarot Atu IX, the Hermit, a consecrated Kamea of Mercury and the four Magical Instruments in their proper places, Cup with water. Ritual Book on stand by chair in west. Black Pillar in northwest corner of room, white Pillar behind chair in west with staff leaning against it. Thurible with charcoal, lighter and incense on stand in south. Incense: dittany of crete. No music. Robed, hooded, girded and sandaled, enter, salute Altar, go deosil lighting Secret Flame and igniting charcoal, go to west, sit. Long pause, hands folded with thumbs touching opposite palms, hood almost covering face. After a while, read aloud:

Path Twenty-One of the Tree of Life is "the Stable Intelligence, and it is so called because it has the virtue of Consistency among all numerations." To this path is assigned the Hebrew letter YOD which means Hand and has the numerical value of 10, the zodiacal sign of Virgo the Virgin, and Tarot Atu IX, the Hermit. The letter Yod means a Hand and indicates means of action. The Hand, being a symbol of creative and directive energy, is a polite equivalent of the Spermatozoon, the true gylph. The letter Yod is the foundation of all the other letters of the Hebrew alphabet which are merely combinations of it in various forms. It is the first letter of Tetragrammaton and thus symbolizes the Father who is Chokmah, Wisdom. Chokmah is the Sphere of the Zodiac and the Sphere of Uranus, Lord of Magic, who is an expression of Universal Mind also symbolized by Mercury, the Magician, ruler of Virgo. The Father's Logos or Word is the Son whose seat and symbol is the Sun. The Son is in the Father and the Father is in the Son. The Son's Logos or Word is Mercury. The Father is the Creator of all worlds through the instrumentality of his Son, his Seed. Accordingly his representative in physical life is the Spermatozoon, true meaning of the letter Yod. This I honor.

Rise, go deosil to south, put incense into thurible and cense Altar, saying:

> *Hail the Yod of Tetragrammaton!*
> *Hail the Son, the Seed of the Father!*
> *Hail Mercury, Ruler of Virgo!*

Replace Censer. Go to west, face Altar, take Tarot Atu IX, the Hermit, hold it high and say:

Prophet of the Eternal! Magus of the Voice of Power! Alone you are, lonely you are not. You hold the Secret Seed of All. Yours is the Secret of the Gate of Initiation. But you are searching for something. What is it you seek? Reveal to me your Mystery! [Lower card and gaze at it for a moment.] *In divination this card signifies illumination from within and practical plans derived accordingly. Reversed, it means retirement from participation in current events. But what is its esoteric significance? What instruction in Magic does the Hermit give me?* [Pause. Again hold high the card.] *"Wander alone; bearing the Light and thy Staff. And be thy Light so bright that no man seeth thee. Be not moved by aught without or within. Keep Silence in all thy ways. The Stillness is All."*

Lower card. Freeze into absolute stillness for a moment, moving not, feeling not, thinking of nothing. Replace card. Touch Kamea of Mercury and say:

Thoth! Tahuti! Hermes! Mercury! Herne! Many-named you are, Divine Intelligence, complex and multifaceted in your nature. What part or facet of your being gives you rulership over Virgo the Virgin? It is easy to see your iridescence, duality, cleverness and dexterity expressing through Gemini. What in Virgo expresses you? [Pause.] *Now Virgo is of the Earth Triplicity, it is water of earth, as fields, quiet to bear vegetable and animal life. It is a Mutable Sign, as liquid earth such as mortar or cement. In human anatomy Virgo rules the bowels, especially the small intestines. The function of the small intestine is to pick out and choose the nutriment which the body needs. This requires statistical, factual, practical, analytical discrimination and ability to do minute detailed work. This is why Mercury rules Virgo, the intelligent and quick one deliberately using the earthiness of Virgo to brake himself to detailed analysis. So the Virtue of this Path is Analysis, a typical Virgoan ability. May this virtue be a part of me! To this I drink.*

Take Cup, offer it, drink, replace Cup. Turn left to face north. Say:

The negative side of analysis is the Virgoan tendency to be super-critical, even fault-finding. Thus the Vice of this Path is Criticism. May this vice be not a part of me!

Make Hexagram of Earth toward the north, (as follows):

In its center draw the astrological symbol of Virgo, saying:

Ararita! Begone, carping criticism, begone! [Turn to Altar.] *The horizon of the north is clear.*

Sit. Pull hood to almost cover face. Fold hands, thumbs touching opposite palms. Head bowed, eyes closed, enter the Silence. After a while stand, take staff, go to Altar, take lamp, walk deosil very slowly and in silence three times around Altar, repeating mentally the magical instructions of the Hermit:

Wander alone; bearing the Light and thy Staff. And be thy Light so bright that no man seeth thee. Be not moved by aught without or within. Keep Silence in all thy ways. The Stillness is All."

Return to west, replace lamp and staff, salute Altar, give Sign of Silence. The Rite is finished.

Generous Giver of Gifts

Optional preliminary: Not a requirement for the performance of the Rite but magically appropriate for it is the wearing of an Amethyst ring on the right forefinger. The ring should previously be exorcised and consecrated according to the Rite of Consecrating Talismans, using the names and titles associated with Jupiter. The Amethyst is a Jupiterian Gem which occultly signifies happiness and wealth, gives courage and keeps from drunkenness.

Time: Waxing Moon on a Thursday, early in the morning, mid-afternoon or late evening.

On Altar are Tarot Atu X, the Wheel of Fortune, a consecrated Kamea of Jupiter, four tall purple or blue candles at the four corners, a profusion of evergreen branches and pine cones or oak leaves and acorns or a bouquet of dahlias or chrysanthemums, and the four Magical Instruments in their proper places, Cup with red wine. Black pillar in northwest corner of room, white pillar in southwest corner. Ritual Book on stand by chair in west. Incense: pine needles or cedar shavings or cedar chips or dried sage or cinquefoil or cinnamon sticks pounded in a mortar and sprinkled with a few drops of almond extract and/or arnica and/or oil of musk and/or oil of civet and/or olive oil and/or saffron. Robed, girded, sandaled and perhaps with Amethyst ring on right forefinger, enter, salute Altar, go deosil lighting candles and igniting charcoal. Go to west, sit. Read aloud:

The Twentieth Path of the Tree of Life is "the Intelligence of Conciliation and is so called because it receives and transmits divine influence as a benediction upon all and each existence." To path Twenty is assigned the planet Jupiter, Tarot Atu X, the Wheel of Fortune, and the Hebrew letter RESH which means head or face. This Path represents the All Father in three forms, Fire, Air and Water.

Stand. Say:

> *Holy art Thou, Lord of the Universe!*
> *Holy art Thou, whom nature hath not formed.*
> *Holy art Thou, the vast and the mighty One.*
> *Lord of the light and of the darkness.*
> *IAO! IAO! IAO!*

Perform Qabalistic Cross. Give Sign of the Enterer. Circumambulate deosil to south, singing:

> *O worship the King all glorious above;*
> *O gratefully sing his power and his love;*
> *Our shield and defender, the Ancient of Days,*
> *Pavilioned in splendor and girded with praise.*

Cast incense into Censer and cense Altar, saying:

> *Kyrie, eleison! (ky-ree, ee-lay-ee-sohn)*
> *Kyrie, eleison*
> *Kyrie, eleison!*

Replace Censer. Go to west. Kneel. Say:

Our Father, Who art in heaven: Hallowed by thy Name. Thy kingdom come, thy will be done in earth as it is in heaven. Give us this day our daily bread; and forgive our trespasses as we forgive those that trespass against us; and lead us not into temptation but deliver us from evil. [Perform Qabalistic Cross.]

Remain on knees in silence for a brief span. Here let one's personal prayers of adoration, praise, thanksgiving and petition be said. Then arise and circumambulate deosil, singing:

O tell of his might, O sing of his grace,
Whose robe is the light, Whose canopy space:
His chariots of wrath the deep thunder clouds form,
And dark is his path on the wings of the storm.

Thy bountiful care what tongue can recite?
It breathes in the air, it shines in the light,
It streams from the hill, it descends to the plain,
And sweetly distills in the dew and the rain.

Frail children of dust and feeble as frail,
In thee do we trust, nor find thee to fail.
Thy mercies how tender, how firm to the end,
Our maker, defender, redeemer and friend.

Finish circumambulation in the west. Touch Kamea of Jupiter and say:

This path leads to and from the fourth holy Sephira, Chesed (Hay-sed), Mercy. It represents the Fatherhood of God, depicting God as the loving father, kind and merciful.

Hold high the Kamea and say:

For I am merciful
Because mine understanding compasseth
The secret nature of all things,
And my loving-kindness is the fruit
Of my discrimination.
It is written;
"The eyes of the Lord are in every place,
Beholding the evil and the good."
And because I,
The Dweller in the House of Chesed,
See all things as they really are,
My vision hath no taint of false judgment.
Seeing, I understand,
And because nothing is hid from me,
Therefore am I merciful.
But the path of my mercy
Is a way concealed from the profane,
Because they have not attained unto my perfect vision.
Easier to follow is the flight of an eagle,
For my way soareth high above the comprehension
Of the mind of man.

Replace Kamea. Pause in contemplation. Then take Tarot Atu X, hold it high and say:

Lord of the Forces of Life! Your magical gift is the Power of Acquiring Ascendency. Reveal to me your Mystery! [Lower card and gaze at it for a moment.] *This is the Wheel of Fortune. Above is the Sphinx combining the four Kerubs, the Bull, the Lion, the Eagle and the Man. The Sphinx asks the Riddle of Existence. To find the Answer I must WILL, KNOW, DARE and BE SILENT. Ascending is Hermanubis. Descending is Typhon. These three figures represent what the Hindus call the Three Gunas. A Guna is a quality, a form of energy. SATTVAS is calm intelligence, lucidity, balance. This is the Sphinx. RAJAS is movement, excitement, fire brilliance, restlessness. This is Hermanubis. TAMAS is darkness, inertia, sloth, ignorance. This is Typhon. A Hindu master saying is, "the Gunas revolve." The Wheel of Fortune illustrates this idea. Its divinatory meaning is a change of fortune, when upright for the better, when reversed for the worse. This card tells me the universe is in a continual state of change. Everything turns into its opposite at one time or another.* [Pause in contemplation. Again elevate card.] *"Sped by its energies triune, the Wheel of Fortune spins, its axle immobile. Follow thy fortune, careless where it leads thee. The axle moveth not; attain thou that."*

Replace card. Pause in contemplation. Take Wand, hold it high and say:

Merciful All Father! Amon Ra! Brahma! Zeus! Jupiter! El! Thine is the Kingdom of goodness and mercy, thou art the King we acknowledge and adore; thine is the Kingdom, thine the power and glory. Praise be to thee, Father, forever more.

Replace Wand. Take Dagger, hold it high and say:

Thine is the power, everlasting, eternal, nor can thy grandeur our feeble minds explore; thine is the kingdom, thine the power and glory. Praise be to thee, Father, forevermore.

Replace Dagger. Take Cup, hold it high and say:

Thine is the glory, transcendent, eternal, thy love alone shall this wand'ring world restore; thine is the kingdom, thine the power and glory. Praise be to thee, Father, forevermore.

Drink. Replace Cup. Say:

The Virtue of this Path is Generosity. Generous may I ever be! On the Noble Eightfold Path this is Right Discipline. Rightly disciplined may I ever be! The Sin of this Path is Gluttony. Gluttonous may I never be! The Vices of this Path are Bigotry, Conceit and Hypocrisy. Hekas! Hekas! Este Bibeloi! Bigotry, conceit and hypocrisy; be far from me, be far from me! In the Name of El, so mote it be!

Sit. Enter the Silence. Perform Closing Exercises of Temple Rite.

The Roar of the Lion

Prerequisite: Knowledge of the influence of the Sun in each Sign of the Zodiac. Knowledge of the influence of Leo occupying the cusp of each house of the horoscope.

Preliminary: If at all possible visit a zoo or menagerie and spend some time studying the lion. Note his majesty and dignity, his poise when at rest, his mysterious gaze which never looks at one but which seemingly sees clear through and beyond the physical man. The lion, more than any other animal, has complete balance between his breathing and his heartbeat. Take a tape recorder with you on the chance of being able to record the lion's roar. Suggested reading: *Deeper Secrets of Human History* and *Man as Symphony of the Creative Word* by Rudolf Steiner.

Time: Waxing Moon in Leo.

On Altar are five tall orange or yellow candles—one in center, one at each corner—a consecrated Kamea of the Sun, Tarot Atu XI, Strength, a bouquet of orange or yellow flowers (sunflowers if

possible) and the four Magical Instruments in their proper places, Cup
with Mint Julep or golden colored brandy.

MINT JULEP

Crush two or three leaves of fresh mint, rub them around inside
Cup and discard them. Put two or three broken mint leaves in
Cup, add two ounces of bourbon whiskey, half fill Cup with
crushed ice, stir until Cup is frosted. Add two or three more
broken mint leaves, two more ounces of the whiskey, fill Cup to
top with crushed ice, garnish with unbroken mint leaves.

Black Pillar is against center of northern wall, white pillar against
center of southern wall. Chair in west, facing east. By it is stand with
Ritual Book. Incense: frankincense. Robed, girded and sandaled,
enter, salute Altar, go deosil lighting candles and igniting charcoal, go
to west, sit. Read aloud:

*The Nineteenth Path of the Tree of Life, connecting Chesed and
Geburah, is "the Luminous Intelligence because by it is perfected the
nature of all things under the Orb of the Sun." To it is assigned the
Hebrew letter ZAIN which means Sword, Tarot Atu XI, Strength, and
the Zodiacal Sign of Leo the Lion ruled by the Sun. In my natal
Horoscope the Sun is in the Sign of _____ occupying the _____ House, with aspects of _____
_____. Thus, my [Houses] and [Aspects] are
influenced by Leo and its ruler the Sun.*

Meditate on the above for a while. Then stand, go to Altar, take Cup
and sip therefrom, replace Cup. Say:

*The Virtue of the Path is Kindness. Kindness is divinity expressed in
the lives of men. Kind may I ever be. The Vice of this Path is
Domination. May the need to dominate be far from me; this is my will
and so mote it be!*

Take another sip from Cup. Then go deosil to south, saying:

Leo is of the fire triplicity. It is air of fire, as sunshine. It is a fixed sign, as hot metal. Leo represents the Act of Power. Leo is ruled by the Sun. In the Sun is the Secret of the Spirit. This I seek.

Cast incense into Censer and cense Altar, saying:

> *Evohe, Apollo, God of Light!*
> *Evohe, Amon-Ra, Lord of the Skies!*
> *Evohe, Sol, Great Sun, Ruler of Leo!*

Replace Censer, go to west, take Cup, sip, replace Cup. Take Tarot Atu XI, Strength, hold it high and say:

Daughter of the Flaming Sword! You are Strength, not strength alone, but the joy of strength exercised! Reveal to me your Mystery! [Lower card and gaze at it for a moment.] *A smiling woman holds the open jaws of a fierce and powerful lion. Is she opening his mouth or closing it?* [Pause.] *She is performing an Act of Power. Whether opening or closing the lion's mouth, she is doing what she chooses to do, she is exercising her will!* [Pause.] *Do what thou wilt shall be the whole of the law!* [Pause.] *But love is the law, love under will.* [Pause.] *She is exercising her will with love. She loves doing her will, expressing her strength. Or strength comes from doing one's will with love. Vigor and the rapture of vigor! Thus she says to me:* [again hold high the card] *"The joy of strength expressed! Mitigate energy with love; but let love devour all things! For love is the law, love under will!"*

Replace card. Pause in meditation. Take another sip from Cup. Touch Kamea of the Sun and say:

Homage to thee, O thou who art Ra when thou riseth and Temmu when thou settest. Thou riseth, thou riseth, thou shinest, thou shinest, thou who art crowned king of the gods. Thou art the lord of heaven, the lord of earth. Worshipped be thou whom the goddess Maat embraceth at morn, and at eve. Thou dost travel across the sky with heart swelling with joy. Thou art crowned prince of heaven, thou art the one dowered with all sovereignty who comest from the sky. Ra is victorious! O thou divine youth, thou heir of everlastingness, the company of the gods rejoice when thou riseth and when thou sailest across the sky!

Replace Kamea. Take sip from Cup. Take Wand and make invoking Pentagram of Fire:

Say:

I invoke the Fixed Fire of Leo!

Make invoking Hexagram of Fire and symbol of Leo, saying:

Ararita! Leo! Leo! Leo! Ararita!

Replace Wand. Take Cup, offer it, saying:

I drink the Fire of Leo! Roar, lion, roar! Proclaim your power!

Sip. Pause and imagine the lion roaring. If you have a tape of a lion's roar, play it now. Finish the drink, replace Cup. Salute the Altar. Give Sign of Silence. The Rite is finished.

• • •

Note: If you are unused to drinking alcohol you may be partially intoxicated. If so, go forth and do a little roaring on your own. But remember, the Theurgist takes the drink, he allows not the drink to take *him*.

Triple Rite of Path Eighteen

The Scorpion, the Snake and the Eagle

Required reading: *Through the Gates of Death* by Dion Fortune. *Many Mansions* by Gina Cerminara. *Spirit Teachings* by W. Stainton Moses. *The Human Personality and Its Survival of Bodily Death* by F. W. H. Myers.

Preliminary: Let the Theurgist make preparation for death by 1) making his will, 2) deciding and telling his next-of-kin how he wants his body disposed of after his death (the Theurgic way is cremation), and 3) deciding and so indicating to responsible others if any and what kind of funeral or memorial service is to be held, where, and conducted by whom.

Prerequisite: Ability to ascertain and to interpret probable consequence of what Zodiacal Signs are on the cusps of houses 4, 8 and 12 of your natal horoscope, what luminaries or planets are in those houses, and what aspects they form.

Time: On three successive nights with Moon in Libra-Scorpio or Scorpio-Sagittarius. If all three parts of the Rite are to be performed the same evening, waxing Moon in Scorpio.

Black Pillar is against center of eastern wall, white Pillar in southeast corner of room. Just west of and in line with the black Pillar is a cot, head eastward. On Altar in center of room is Tarot Atu XIII, Death, with a sprig of acacia or evergreen beside it, a bouquet of white flowers, tall white candles at the four corners, and the four Magical Instruments in their proper places, Cup with water, Natal Horoscope and Ritual Book on stand by chair in west. Incense: myrrh.

THE SCORPION

Robed, hooded, girded and sandaled, perform Opening Exercise of Temple Rite, igniting the charcoal at the time of lighting the candles and censing the Altar after the sign of the Enterer. Seated in the west, read aloud:

Before me is Path Eighteen of the Tree of Life, connecting Geburah and Binah. Path Eighteen is "the Intelligence of Probation, or is Tentative, and is so called because it is the primary temptation by which the Creator trieth all righteous persons." To this Path is assigned the Hebrew letter TETH which means Serpent. Also assigned here is Tarot Atu XIII, Death, and the Zodiacal Sign of Scorpio. In my natal horoscope _____ degrees of Scorpio occupy the Cusp of the _____ House. In Scorpio is/are [planets] making these aspects _____ There are three types of Scorpio symbolized by the Scorpion, the Snake, and the Eagle. The lower, the Scorpion, is subject to environment, extraordinarily sensitive and responsive to its environment, willingly subjects itself to change. Scorpio is of the Water Triplicity; it is Air of Water, as ocean currents and waves, steady force. It is a fixed Sign, as liquid crystallized through pressure. Many Astrologers consider Scorpio to be the most intense of all the Signs of the Zodiac.

Stand and perform the L. V. X. Signs.

THE L. V. X. SIGNS

Facing east, stand upright, feet together, left arm at side, right forearm across body at diaphragm. Say:

I. N. R. I.
Yod, Nun, Resh, Yod.
Virgo, Isis, Mighty Mother.
Scorpio, Apophis, destroyer.
Sol, Osiris, Slain and Risen.
Isis, Apophis, Osiris, IAO.

Extend the arms to either side so as to make your body a cross. Say:

The Sign of Osiris Slain.

Raise the right arm to point upward, keeping the elbow square, lower the left arm to point downward, keeping the elbow square, while turning the head over the left shoulder looking down so that the eyes follow the left forearm. Say:

The Sign of the Mourning of Isis.

Raise the arms at an angle of sixty degrees to each other above the head which is thrown back, and say:

The Sign of Apophis and Typhon.

Cross the arms on the breast so that the extended fingers almost touch the opposite shoulder, bow the head, and say:

The Sign of Osiris Risen.

Extend the arms again as in Sign of Osiris Slain and cross them again as in the Sign of Osiris Risen, saying:

L. V. X., Lux, the Light of the cross.

Then circumambulate deosil to east, face Altar, trace Hexagram of Water toward the west. Extend ring finger, other fingers clasped toward palm by thumb. With extended finger draw the hexagram in the air before you by connecting the periods 1 to 4, then a to d.

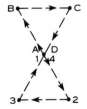

Say: *Ararita.*

Trace symbol of Scorpio, saying:

Scorpio! Scorpio! Scorpio! Ararita!

Return deosil to west, sit. Read aloud:

I am now in Scorpio, resourceful, creative, introverted, secretive, with strong emotions and an affinity with liquids. Resourcefulness is the Virtue of this Path. This virtue I desire. Resourcefulness! Be part of me, and as I will, so mote it be! Scorpio rules the sex parts, symbolic of creativity. [Touch private parts.] *Strong, strong is the power in me to strongly, strongly creative be! Scorpio is often turned within itself.* [Pull hood to partly cover face.] *What do you seek within, O Soul, my brother, what do you seek within? I seek a life that shall never die, some haven to win from mortality. Secretive often Scorpio is, may my ability equal his!* [Sign of Silence.] *Scorpio people are famous for their strong emotions. Mars! Lord of Strength! Pluto! Strong Lord of the Underworld! Make my emotions strong and deep, and may them so I ever keep! Scorpio has affinity with water.*

Rise, go to Altar, take Cup, hold it high and say:

I drink to and take within myself to be a part of me these Scorpio qualities which I have named.

Drink. Replace Cup. Go deosil to east, face Altar and say:

But the Vice of this Path is Troublesomeness. This manifests in the Scorpion phase of Scorpio as jealousy, love of revenge and of argument, an incessant desire to oppose and to fight, to be obstinate and to hate. A negative Scorpio weakness is a tendency to dissipation. Am I jealous and why? [Pause in consideration.] *Am I revengeful, argumentative, obstinate?* [Pause in consideration.] *Do I have a lot of hate in me? Am I often full of hate?* [Pause in consideration.] *If so, that makes me a hateful person. Do I have a tendency to dissipation? Am I dissipated?* [Pause in consideration.] *Whatever amount of these negative Scorpion weaknesses of Scorpio I may have I want them not and banished be they, far, far from me.*

Visualize a scorpion on chair in west. Take Wand and make counterclockwise circle around the thought-form, saying:

Hekas! Hekas! Este Bibeloi! Be far from here, O ye profane! Be ever, ever far from me; and as I will, so mote it be! [Replace Wand.] *The circle of Fire has destroyed the Scorpion. Clean is the seat in the west.*

Go to west, sit. Read aloud:

The natural House of Scorpio in the Horoscope is the Eighth which among other things, is the House of Death. In my natal chart the Sign of _____ is on the Cusp of the Eighth House and in my Eighth House is (are) [planets] with aspects of _____ _____

Lower hood still farther over face, bow head. Fold hands with thumbs touching opposite palms. Long pause. Then raise hood just enough to read:

Man that is born of woman is of few days, and full of trouble. The days of our years are threescore and ten, and if by reason of strength given by Mars or Pluto they be fourscore years, yet is their strength labor and sorrow, for it is soon cut off, and we fly away. All that liveth, dieth. I live. I shall die. By what cause? When? Under what circumstances? Who will be with me when I die? Adonai, my Lord, will be with me, I know. Adonai, my Lord, abide with me!

Stand. Slowly circumambulate deosil to cot, singing:

> *Abide with me! Fast falls the eventide;*
> *The darkness deepens; Lord, with me abide!*
> *When other helpers fail, and comforts flee,*
> *Help of the helpless, O abide with me!*

> *Swift to its close ebbs out life's little day:*
> *Earth's joys grow dim, its glories pass away;*
> *Change and decay in all around I see;*
> *O thou who changest not, abide with me!*

Having come to the cot, divest yourself of hooded robe, girdle and sandals, saying:

Naked came I into the world. Naked let me go out.

Lie on cot, head eastward, hands clasped behind head, right ankle under left knee, eyes closed. Think of your death; imagine the various diseases that may attack you, or accidents overtake you. Vividly visualize and feel the process of the death of your physical body. Enter the Silence, becoming absolutely still, utterly quiet. Several minutes or several hours will pass. Afterward simply get dressed and go about your usual business.

THE SNAKE

Temple set-up same as above but fresh water for the flowers if needed, fresh water in Cup, fresh candles, charcoal, incense. Robed, girded and sandaled, enter, salute Altar, go deosil lighting candles and igniting charcoal, go to west, sit. Read aloud:

This Eighteenth Path of the Tree of Life has a Snake as one of its symbols. The Snake phase of Scorpio is alternately subject to inner impulses and outer stimuli. The problem of this phase of Scorpio is emotional control. The emotions, being strong, sometimes get out of hand. Do I have this problem? [Pause in consideration.] *May my emotions be ever strong, but ever may I keep them firmly under control. I must have them, they must not have me! This is my will; and so mote it be! The bad karma of this phase of Scorpio is to think it is always right, whether or not it is right. This is arrogance, lack of judgement, no true sense of values. Is this a fault of mine? Do I think I am always right?* [Pause in consideration.] *From the sins of false pride and arrogance, Good Lord deliver me!*

Head up with eyes closed, back straight and not touching back of chair, knees together, hands palms down on thighs or knees, become tense all over as you take an extra-deep breath and hold it for a long time. Then audibly exhale through the mouth and relax. Read aloud:

Since ancient times, because of the shedding of its skin the snake has been symbolic of regeneration and reincarnation. Of course it is also a phallic symbol and Scorpio rules the sex organs. May the holy rites of the Paths of the Tree refresh, make clean, and regenerate me! Many lives I have lived, many more are yet to come! Through them all may the power of sex be strong in me!

Repeat posture, tensing, holding breath, exhaling and relaxing as above. Then say:

At death I shed this body as the snake his skin. This physical body that sits here is not me, it is mine. These emotions that feel are not me, they are mine. This mind that thinks is not me, it is mine. Who then and what am I, the I that thinks with the mind, the I that feels with the emotions, the I that resides in the physical body?

Stand. Go deosil to south, cast incense into the Censer and cense Altar, saying:

> Evohe, Evohe Monad!
> Evohe, Evohe, Atman!
> Evohe, Evohe, Spirit!

Replace Censer. Go to west, take Tarot Atu XIII, Death, hold it high and say:

Lord of the Gate of Death! Child of the Great Transformers! Most people dread and avoid you. Are you to be feared? Are you to be shunned? Reveal to me your Mystery!

Lower card to eye level, gaze at if for a moment. Then say:

This card represents transformation, change, voluntary or involuntary, in either case logical development of existing conditions, yet perhaps sudden and unexpected. Apparent death or destruction, yet such interpretation is illusion. [Pause in reflection. Again hold card high and say:] *"The Universe is Change; every Change is the effect of an Act of Love; all Acts of Love contain Pure Joy. Die daily. Death is the apex of one curve of the snake Life; behold all opposites as necessary complements, and rejoice. Initiation is guarded on both sides by Death."*

Pause in contemplation. Replace card on Altar. Take Cup and hold it high, saying:

Death is but a change, a transformation from the physical to the non-physical, from the lower to the higher, from the outer to the inner, from time to timelessness. What about my loved ones who have gone before me through the change of death to "over there," the "beyond," the next phase of life, the spirit world? Will I see them again? Who will be waiting for me when I go over? Pluto! Lord of Death! Let me see the other side! Hermes Psychopomp, Leader of Souls! Show me the way!

Go to cot, remove clothing and sandals, lie down. With thumb of right hand make Circled Cross [up to down, right to left, then clockwise circle] on forehead between eyebrows, saying:

Eye of Spirit! Open!

Clasped hands behind head, right ankle under left knee, eyes closed, vividly visualize your own death but from the non-physical rather than the physical point of view. Who, from the other side, is there to meet you? Enter the Silence, becoming perfectly still, utterly quiet. Several minutes to several hours will pass. Afterward get dressed and go about your usual business.

THE EAGLE

Temple as above except for fresh water, candles, charcoal and incense. Robed, girded and sandaled, enter Temple, salute Altar, go deosil lighting candles and charcoal, go to west, sit. Read aloud:

High soars the Eagle! The Eagle soars high! On this Eighteenth Path of the Tree of Life the Eagle represents exaltation above materiality. Fly high, O Soul of me, become the Eagle flying high! Let me see Scorpio and Death from an exalted point of view!

Stand. Circumambulate deosil to south, put incense in Thurible and cense Altar, saying:

> *Lord of Death!*
> *Lord of Life!*
> *The Lord is One.*

Replace Censer. Go deosil to east. Take sprig of acacia or evergreen, hold it high and say:

> *Never the spirit was born!*
> *The spirit shall cease to be never!*
> *Never was time it was not;*
> *End and beginning are dreams.*
> *Birthless and deathless and changeless*
> *Abideth the spirit forever;*
> *Death can not touch it at all,*
> *Dead though the house of its seems.*

Return sprig to Altar. Go deosil to west. Take Cup and say:

> *A stone I died and rose again a plant,*
> *A plant I died and rose an animal;*
> *I died an animal and was born a human.*
> *Why should I fear? What have I lost by death?*

Hold high the Cup and say:

The soul of a person
Is like water;
From heaven it cometh,
To heaven it mounteth,
And thence again
It must back to earth,
Forever changing.

Drink. Replace Cup. Circumambulate deosil while saying:

Nay, but as when a man layeth
His worn-out robes away,
And taking new ones, sayeth,
These will I wear today;
So putteth by the spirit
Lightly its garb of flesh,
And passeth to inherit
A residence afresh.

Go to cot, remove clothing and sandals, lie with hands clasped behind head. right ankle under left knee, eyes closed. Become absolutely quiet, utterly still. Imagine total darkness. Then vividly visualize yourself standing in a glorious globe of rose and gold. Hear the beating of Eagles' wings. Let your standing self cry triumphantly, "Evohe!" Then visualize that standing Self sink down upon the cot. Rest for awhile. Get up, dress, perform Closing Exercises of Temple Rite.

The Chariot of Life

Time: Waxing Moon In Cancer.

Black pillar in northeast corner of room. Before it, facing southwest, is stand with statue or picture of Madonna and Child which may be Isis with the infant Horus or Mary with the baby Jesus, with white candles on either side and a consecrated Kamea of the Sun lying before it. Altar in center of room so placed its eastern side faces northeast corner of room. On Altar are Tarot Atu VII, the Chariot, and Cup with water containing a small piece of gold such as a gold coin or gold ring or, best of all, a gold nugget. If gold is unavailable then a single golden colored flower such as a marigold may be substituted. Four tall white candles at the four corners of the Altar and, if desired and available, a profusion of water-lily, lotus, lily or white gladiolus or any white flower whose shape suggests a chalice or cup. Kamea of the Moon with Ritual Book on stand by chair in west. White pillar in southwest corner of room. Incense: myrrh. Robed, girded and sandaled, enter, salute Altar, go deosil lighting candles and igniting charcoal, go to west, sit. Read aloud:

The Seventeenth Path of the Tree of Life is "the Disposing Intelligence which provides Faith to the Righteous and they are clothed with the Holy Spirit by it, and it is called the Foundation of Excellence in the state of higher things." [Pause in contemplation.] *To Path Seventeen is assigned the Hebrew letter TZADDI which means Fish Hook, the Zodiacal Sign of Cancer the Crab, and Tarot Atu VII, the Chariot. The Seventeenth Path connects Binah and Tiphareth. Binah is the Mother. Tiphareth is the Child. Thus Path Seventeen is the Mother-Child relationship. My mother's maiden name was _____ . She married my father when she was _____ years old. I am her _____ child. I remember* [mother, mama, ma, mom, whatever word you used for and to her] *and I* [here remember, visualize and name your own special activities and relationships with your mother.] *I honor her. She conceived me. She carried me in her womb. She opened the Door of Life for me in this incarnation. I honor her.* [Stand. Say:] *Blessed be* [full name of your mother].

Go deosil to south. Put incense into Censer and cense Altar, saying:

Hail Isis, Lady of Love!
Hail Mary, Full of Grace!
Hail Binah, Supernal Mother!

Replace Censer. Go deosil to west, take Tarot Atu, hold it high and say:

Lord of the Triumph of Light! Child of the Powers of the Waters! Reveal to me your Mystery! [Lower card and gaze at it for a moment.] *I see a chariot drawn by two sphinxes, a white and a black. Four pillars support a sky-blue canopy spangled with five-pointed stars. Beneath the canopy stands a young and holy king. He carries the sceptre of solar energy and his shoulders are ornamented with lunar crescents. A seven-pointed star shines on his crown. On the front of the chariot is fastened a two-winged sphere and a mystic lingam and yoni, the symbol of union. It is said that everything in this picture has a meaning so I don't want to miss anything. Towers of a walled town— the chariot's body seems to be silver with wheels of gold—a square upon his breast—there are no reins—anything else?* [Pause, gazing at card.] *In divination, when this card is upright it means triumph or victory; reversed it means ruthlessness and love of destruction.* [Pause to memorize.] *What is its esoteric meaning?* [Again hold card high.] *The Issue of the Two-in-One, Chokmah-Binah, conveyed; this is the Chariot of Power.*

Replace card. Pause in contemplation. Then take up Cup and carry it to the stand in northeast corner and place it on the Kamea of the Sun. Kneel before the Madonna and Child. Say:

Great Mother! Anima Mundi, Soul of the World! Thou art the Motherhood of God. Thee, thee, I invoke! Thou art the Lady with ten thousand appellations. Thou art Marah, the Great Sea. Thou art the First He of Tetragrammaton. Thou art Queen of Heaven. Thee, thee I adore!

Prostrate yourself completely, lying face down upon the floor, both arms outstretched. Remain so for several moments. Then arise, take Cup and hold it high, saying:

The Pregnant Womb receiving and holding Life. The Golden Child is conceived.

Holding Cup close to your heart circumambulate deosil the Altar, saying:

I am the Chariot of Power conveying the Issue of the Two-in One. The Canopy of the Great Mother is over you, Golden Child! Remember, remember—Following her, thou strayest not; invoking her, thou despairest not; thinking of her, thou wanderest not; upheld by her, thou growest not weary; favored by her, thou reachest the goal.

Replace Cup on altar from its western side. Sit. Enter the Silence. After a while, read aloud:

Three aspects has the Great Mother. The first is the Door of Life. The second is Aima (ah-ee-mah) the bright fertile Mother. This is Isis the Bright Mother, Mary the Holy Mother, and all the mothers of the Savior Gods, the Holy Avatars, of all the great Astrological Ages. The third is Ama (ah-mah) the dark sterile Mother. This is Nephthys the Dark Mother and all cruel and unnatural mothers expressing the negative qualities of the Chariot and Cancer. [Touch Kamea of the Moon.] This Path has assigned to it the Sign of Cancer ruled by the Moon. Ordinarily we think of the Moon as having two phases, waxing and waning. But really the Moon has three phases, waxing, full and waning, corresponding to the three aspects of the Great Mother. Cancer is the mother sign. It gives the desire to take care of whatever is in need of nurture; its inner urge is maternal in men as well as women. The nourishing love principle is the special quality of the Cancer native, for innate is the urge and desire to feed and tend others. Cancer is related to the Moon's sphere and the Moon rules the Astral which is exceedingly mobile—of terrific speed and intensely rapid transformation. It is so formative and plastic that it is easy to understand why one is restless and changeable when under the Moon and Cancer. The physical counterpart of the lunar sphere is the sea, and all water comes under the rule of Cancer. The desire of Cancer, its thirst, is for feeling, and to live in an emotional ocean of sensation, to touch everything and everyone through the astral senses. Let me experience the Sign of Cancer.

Take Kamea of the Moon in left hand. Stand. With Third or Ring finger of right hand make Hexagram of Water and as if within it the symbol of Cancer, saying:

Ararita! Cancer! Cancer! Cancer! Ararita!

Become very passive. Psychically "tune-in" as you slowly circumambulate deosil. Returned to the west, replace Kamea, face Altar and say:

The Virtue of this Path is Tenacity. Positively and selectively tenacious may I ever be. The Vice of this Path is Touchiness. Negatively and indiscriminately sensitive may I never be. Such is my will and so mote it be! [Pause.] *I drink to the Mother and Child.*

Take Cup, offer it, drink, replace Cup. Salute the Altar and give Sign of Silence. The Rite is finished.

The Sign of the Bull

Required reading: *The Gospel According to St. Luke.*

Prerequisite: Experience in hard physical labor.

Time: Waxing Moon in Taurus.

On the Altar is the Disk, the Pentacle, in the center, if possible on a bed of moss edged by daisies. The other Magical Instruments are in their usual places, Cup filled to the brim with water. Also on Altar are Tarot Atu V, the Hierophant, a consecrated Kamea of Venus, and a scattering of bits of alabaster, and/or white coral and/or agate and/or common white pebbles. White pillar behind chair in west. Beside chair is stand with Ritual Book. Black Pillar in northwest corner of room. Incense: storax if possible, otherwise dittany of crete. Robed, girded and sandaled, enter, salute Altar, go deosil to south, ignite charcoal, go to west, sit. Read aloud:

The Sixteenth Path of the Tree of Life is "the Triumphal or Eternal Intelligence, so called because it is the pleasure of the Glory beyond which is no other Glory like it, and it is called also Paradise for the Righteous." [Pause.] *Path Sixteen connects Chokmah and Chesed, hence is on the Pillar of Mercy. To it is assigned the Hebrew letter VAU which means Nail, the Zodiacal Sign of Taurus the Bull, and Tarot Atu V, the Hierophant.*

Stand. Go deosil to south, put incense in Thurible and cense Altar, saying:

> *Hail Apis, Bull of Khem!*
> *Hail Shiva, Sacred Bull!*
> *Hail Auriel, Archangel of Earth!*

Replace Censer. Go to west, take Tarot card, hold it high and say:

Magus of the Eternal! Triumphal One! You are Authority and the Strength of Authority. Reveal to me your Mystery! [Lower card and gaze at it for a moment.] *I see the Great Master in the Temple. He is seated on a throne set upon a dais between the Pillars. He wears the robe of a high priest and a golden tiara. His right hand is raised in the Sign of Esoteric Benediction* [thumb and first two fingers extended, third and little fingers collapsed to palm] *and in his left hand he holds a triple-beamed cross. Under his feet are two crossed keys. Two tonsured priests are kneeling before him, one's robe is embroidered with roses, the other's with lilies. He speaks to them.* [Pause, listen.] *I hear the sound of his voice but can not understand one word that he says. Either he speaks in a language unknown to me or there is something that prevents me from understanding the meaning of his words.* [Pause.] *"He speaks only for those who have ears to hear. But woe unto them who believe that they hear before they have really heard, or hear that which he does not say, or put their own words in place of his words. They will never receive the keys of understanding. And it is said of them that they neither go in themselves, neither suffer them that are entering to go in."* [Pause Kneel.] *Adonai, my Lord, give me ears to hear. Let me not presumptuous be. May I receive the Keys to the Kingdom.* [Remain on knees for a long moment, then stand.] *In divination, when upright this card means established authority, the establishment, strength of position, that which endures. Also it means benevolent rule for the good of all, help from superiors, explanation, instruction. Reversed, it means the establishment that has lost sight of* its true purpose and is no longer fulfilling that purpose, the establishment which has become power-intoxicated and exercises power only to retain that power and so becomes oppressive, the entrenched establishment that is fighting to survive, using fair means and foul. An old name for this card is "The Pope," so it can stand for any established religion, government or power-structure which has lost sight of its true purpose and became oppressive. [Pause to memorize and to contemplate.] But what says the Hierophant to me for my own personal growth in Magic? [Again elevate card.] "Offer thy self Virgin to the Knowledge and Conversation of thine own Holy Guardian Angel. All else is a snare. Submit thyself to Discipline. Labor!

Replace card. Pause in contemplation. Take up Disk and, carrying it, circumambulate deosil while singing or saying:

> To my work! To my work!
> I'm a servant of God.
> Let me follow the Path that my Master has trod.
> In the balm of his counsel my strength to renew,
> Let me do with my might what my hands find to do.
> Toiling on! Toiling on! Toiling on! Toiling on!
> Let me watch,
> Let me wait,
> And labor till the Master comes!

Return to west, examine the Disk as if you are seeing it for the first time. Say:

The Disk is the Magical Instrument of the Earth and is a Pentacle. It symbolizes firmness, concreteness, stability, strength, patience, endurance, practicality, materiality. It is divided into four compartments signifying Fire of Earth, Water of Earth, Air of Earth and Earth of Earth. This Sixteenth Path has Taurus assigned to it. Now Taurus is of the Earth triplicity, it is Air of Earth, as broad plains, steady force. It is a Fixed Sign, like frozen earth, therefore stubborn. It is said that Taurus is the Keeper of the King's Treasure, therefore a Taurean trait is possessiveness, a desire to possess people as well as things, a trait that can degenerate into greediness. But above all else, Taurus is the hard working one, the Toiler.

With Disk make Hexagram of Earth and in its center the symbol of Taurus, saying:

Ararita! Taurus! Taurus! Taurus! Ararita!

Replace Disk. Pause and imagine the pawing and snorting of a bull. Feel yourself becoming strong as he, especially in the neck and shoulders. Then imitate the bull in a slow dance deosil around Altar. Return to the west, touch Kamea of Venus and say:

Venus! Ruler of Taurus! Lady of Graciousness and Luck! Lesser Benefic! May I have the good qualities of Taurus. May I be blessed with Endurance. Remove from me any and all traits of stubbornness, obstinacy, over-possessiveness, greed. This is my will, and with thine aid so mote it be! I drink as the bull drinks.

Bend over and drink from Cup without handling it. Salute the Altar and give Sign of Silence. The Rite is finished.

The Ruler of the Balance

Time: Waxing Moon in Libra.

On center of Altar is a pair of balancing scales. Beside it is Tarot Atu VIII, Justice. The sword used in the Rite of Path Twenty-two is in place of the Dagger, the other three Magical Instruments are in their usual places, Cup with water. White pillar in southwest corner of room with stand before it on which is a potted aloe plant and a consecrated Kamea of Saturn. Black pillar in northwest corner with stand before it on which is another potted aloe plant and a consecrated Kamea of Venus. Ritual Book on stand by chair in west. Incense: galbanum if possible, otherwise dried rose petals. In either case, add a drop of semen or blood. Robed, girded and sandaled, enter, salute Altar, go deosil to south, ignite charcoal, go to west, sit. Read aloud:

The Fifteenth Path of the Tree of Life is "the Intelligence of the Secret of All Spiritual Activities, and is so called because of the affluence diffused by it from the most high blessing." To this Path is assigned the Hebrew letter HE which means Window, the Zodiacal Sign of Libra the Scales, and Tarot Atu VIII, Justice. The Fifteenth Path connects Chokmah and Tiphareth. Chokmah is the Father, Tiphareth is the Child, hence Path Fifteen is the father-child relationship. My father's name is _____. He was _____ years old when I was born. I am his _____ child. I remember [father, pa, papa, dad, daddy, whatever name you used to and for him] *and I* [here remember, name and visualize special activities and relationships you had with your father]. *I honor him. He gave me life. I am the growth of his seed. The child is in the father and the father is in the child. I honor him.* [Stand. Say:]

Blessed be (full name of your father).

Go deosil to south, put incense into censer and cense Altar, saying:

Evohe Venus, ruler of Libra!
Evohe Saturn, exalted therein!
Evohe Raphael, Archangel of Air!

Replace Censer. Go to west. Take Tarot card, hold it high and say:

Daughter of the Lords of Truth! Lady of the Balance! Reveal to me your Mystery! [Lower card and gaze at it for a moment.] *A purple veil hangs between the two Pillars. Before it sits a gold-crowned woman clothed in red robe and green mantle. In her right hand she holds an upward-pointing sword, in her left hand a pair of scales.* [Pause.] *Her look is infinitely deep and terrible, she draws me like an abyss. I tremble.* [Pause.] *"You are seeing Truth. Everything is weighed in those scales. That sword is eternally lifted in defense of justice and nothing can escape it. But why do you turn your eyes from the scales and the sword? Are you afraid? Yes, they deprive you of your illusions. How will you live on earth without illusions? You wished to see Truth and now you see her. But remember what awaits a mortal when he has seen the Goddess. He will never again be able to shut his eyes to what does not please him, as he has done hitherto. Can you bear this? You have seen truth. Now you have to go further even if you do not wish to."* [Pause in consternation and contemplation.] *In divination this card means Justice, or rather, Justesse, the act of adjustment; suspension of action pending decision; in material matters may refer to law suits or prosecutions, in business and social life it refers to contracts, agreements, partnership or marriage settlements or divorce, politically to treaties. Upright, it is favorable to the querent, reversed it is unfavorable.* [Pause to memorize.] *But what esoteric message has Justice for me?* [Again elevate card.] *"By equilibrium and self-sacrifice is the gate. Balance against each thought its exact opposite, for the marriage of these is the annihilation of illusion."*

Replace card. Pause in meditation. Touch scales and say:

Balance against each thought its exact opposite. What, for instance? Up, down; near, far; in, out; war, peace; summer, winter; success, failure; youth, old age; light, darkness; male, female; life, death; head, foot; good, evil. [Add more pairs of opposites of your own choosing.] *The marriage of these is the annihilation of illusion. Does this mean that everything is relative? I remember the occult doctrine, "The myriad pairs of opposites contend not, rather do they co-habit and co-operate to produce the phenomena of the universe." I also remember the saying, "The entire secret of the Occult is the Knowledge of Equilibrium." But before equilibrium can be* attained, *balance must be maintained.* [Go to southeast and bring Kamea of Saturn to the Altar.] *Old One of the night of Time! Greater Malefic!* [Go to northwest and bring Kamea of Venus to the Altar.] *Youthful Lady of Graciousness and Love! Lesser Benefic!*[Put Kameas on pans of scales.] *Help me, I pray, to achieve and maintain* balance *in my life.*

Circumambulate deosil in an ellipse from west of Altar to southeast corner where give Sign of Enterer, to east of Altar, to northwest corner where give Sign of Silence, to west of Altar where stop and say:

The life of my father's sperm fertilized the egg of my mother. In the darkness of her womb the substance of creation combined his and her genes to form this physical body of mine. Carrying the Scales of Karma and the Sword of Nemesis representing the ultimate automatic justice of Nature, I donned the swaddling band of that thick darkness. Since then the Sword has pricked me many times, inflicting wounds. But there is healing in the aloe-juice of this Path, for the healing of all wounds resides in either or both Chokmah and Tiphareth since the Father is in the Son and the Son is in the Father and the Mother is in the Daughter and the Daughter is in the Mother.

Sit. Enter the Silence. After a while, say:

Libra the Scales, assigned to this Path, is of the Air triplicity: it is Fire of Air, as wind, the swift onset of force. It is a cardinal Sign, as gusts of wind. Librans are good companions who need companionship,

*socially conscious and capable, good balancers ever seeking balance,
psychic and perceptive. Let me experience Libra the Scales, sign of
the Autumnal Equinox.*

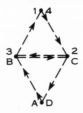

Stand. Take sword and with it make Hexagram of Air and as if within
its center the symbol of Libra, saying:

Ararita! Libra! Libra! Libra! Ararita!

Replace sword. Take scales and carry them deosil once around Altar,
opening yourself psychically. Return to west, replace scales, again
take sword and holding it upright, say:

The Virtue, of this Path is Affability. Affable may I ever be!

Turn sword point downward and say:

*The Vice of this Path is Love of Approbation. May such be forever
banished from me!*

Replace sword. Take Cup, offer it, saying:

Joy to all Librans everywhere!

Drink. Replace Cup. Salute the Altar and give Sign of Silence. The
Rite is finished.

Great One of the Night of Time

Time: Saturday night.

On center of Altar is a single black or grey candle, Tarot Atu XXI, the World, a consecrated Kamea of Saturn, a ball-point pen with black ink, and a small piece of lead such as a lead sinker used by fishermen. If desired, these may be surrounded by a wreath of yew, elm, evergreen or night-blooming flowers. The four Magical Instruments are in their usual places, Cup with sherry wine. Black pillar against center of northern wall, white pillar against center of southern wall. Ritual Book on stand by chair in west. Incense: scammony if possible, otherwise dittany of crete. Robed, hooded, girded and sandaled, enter, salute Altar, go deosil lighting candle and charcoal, go to west, sit. Long pause, head bowed, folded hands in lap with thumb tips touching opposite palms. Then read aloud:

The Fourteenth Path of the Tree of Life is "the Uniting Intelligence and is so named because it is itself the Essence of Glory. It is the Consummation of the Truth of individual spiritual things." It unites

Chokmah and Binah, the Supernal Father and Mother, the Divine Male and Female. Thus its God-Name is Yahweh-Elohim, the Father and Mother eternally conjoined. The uniting is the Essence of Glory and this forms the Holy Sephira, Daath, Knowledge, which has no number and which is not depicted on the Tree of Life because it is always on another level of being and consciousness than that on which one is functioning. [Pause in contemplation.] *To Path Fourteen is assigned the Hebrew letter CHETH which means Fence or Field. A fence is a barrier but also a protector. It marks a boundary, hence suggests limitation. As a fence, Path Fourteen edges the great Abyss and separates the Three Above from the Seven below. A field is thought of as an area of cultivation or a place of work or play. Path Fourteen is the field of Time in which the Father-Mother God works and loves, for it is the Path of their union.* [Pause in contemplation.] *Also assigned to this Path is Tarot Atu XXI, the World, and the planet Saturn. The Virtues of the Fourteenth Path are Orderliness and System. May these virtues ever be mine. On the Noble Eightfold Path this is Right Recollection. May such be mine, may such be mine. The Sin of this Path is Avarice. Its Vice is Selfishness. Avarice and selfishness be far from me; and as I will, so mote it be!* [Pause.] *I honor the Lord of Path Fourteen.*

Stand. Go deosil to south, put incense in Censer and cense Altar, saying:

> *Evohe! Evohe! Kronos!*
> *Evohe! Evohe! Saturn!*
> *Evohe! Evohe! Yahweh-Elohim!*

Replace Censer. Go to west, take Tarot card, hold it high and say:

Great One of the Night of Time! Reveal to me your Mystery! [Lower card and gaze at it for a moment.] *Framed by a wreath of greenery is the dancing figure of a young and beautiful woman, wrapped in a blue scarf, with a magic wand in each hand. In the four corners of the picture are the Kerubic symbols, the heads of a Bull, a Lion, an Eagle and a Man. The background is sky-blue.* [Visualize.] *The girl whirls and the wreath revolves in ever increasing speed.* [Close eyes for a moment and listen.] *I hear far-away music and soft singing and still farther away peals of thunder and the roar of a hurricane and the noise of mountain avalanches and the rumble of earthquakes. Then a strange stillness.* [Pause to experience.] *What does it mean?* [Pause to consider.] *"It is the image of the World. Try to understand that this is the World in the circle of Time amid the Four Principles."* [Pause to reflect.] *The divinatory significance of this card is the end of the matter, the final outcome of the question or problem. Upright, the eventual solution will be satisfactory to the querent. Reversed, the outcome will be unsatisfactory. What is its significance in Magic?* [Again lift card high.] *"Treat Time and all conditions of event as servants of Thy Will, appointed to present the universe to thee in the form of thy Plan."*

Replace card. Touch Kamea of Saturn and say:

Saturn! Terrible things are said of you—that you emasculated your own father and swallowed your own children. In Astrology you are called a Malefic, a bringer of imbalance, pain and sorrow. It is said of you that you are cold, constrictive and obstructive. So the human tendency is to fear and shun you. We picture you, especially at New Year, as Father Time, an old man with a scythe. It is time that emasculates all men and swallows all its children. But you are also the baby of each new year. And the Tarot pictures you with an evergreen wreath surrounding a beautiful dancing girl. And you are the healer of all wounds, the solver of all problems, that which brings all things to birth—and death—and rebirth. You are Lord of Karma!

Lift Kamea high and say:

> *Etherial Father, mighty Titan, hear,*
> *Great sire of gods and men, whom all revere;*
> *Endu'd with various counsel, pure and strong,*
> *To whom increase and decrement belong.*
> *Hence matter's flowing forms thro' thee that die,*
> *By thee restor'd, their former place supply.*
> *O Great Saturn, of a subtle mind,*
> *Propitious hear, to suppliant pray'rs inclin'd.*
> *This sacred rite benevolent attend,*
> *And grant a blameless life, a blessed end.*

Replace Kamea. Take pen and draw symbol of Saturn on palm of left hand, replace pen. Middle and ring finger of left hand held to palm by thumb, forefinger and little finger extended, raise left arm in salute and say:

The Sign of the Old One! Great and powerful is he. Powerful in Magic is his Sign.

Lower arm. Take the piece of lead and carry it deosil around Altar, saying:

Saturn's lead is a heavy metal and symbolizes solidity, stability, crystallization. Saturn rules the Sign of Capricorn, in the human body he rules the skeleton and excretory system. He rules time, antiques and old people. "Grow old along with me, the best is yet to be." I am not afraid of Saturn but I am in awe of him. I accept him as teacher and friend.

Return to the west, replace the piece of lead. Take Cup, offering it, saying:

To the Lord of Time!

Drink. Replace Cup. Salute the Altar and give Sign of Silence. The Rite is finished.

Rite of Path Thirteen

Channel of Scintillating Flame

Required Reading: *The Gospel According to St. Mark.*

Time: Waxing Moon in a Fire Sign.

On the Altar is Tarot Atu XX, Judgement, flanked by two tall white candles. Four tall white candles are at the corners of the Altar and the four Magical Instruments are in their usual places, Cup with small amount of golden colored brandy. Three tall white candles on stand in east. Black Pillar against center of northern wall, before it is stand with two tall white candles. Opposite it against southern wall is white Pillar and stand with two tall white candles. Ritual Book on stand by chair in west. Incense: frankincense.

Fast for twenty-four hours before the Rite, taking only a little water. After bathing, put drop of oil of musk on forehead, lips, back of neck, throat, each shoulder, heart, palms of hands, genitals, back of each knee and soles of feet. Robed, girded and barefoot, enter, salute Altar, go deosil lighting the candles and igniting the charcoal, go to west, sit. Read aloud:

*Thirteen flames and thirteen drops of oil herald the Thirteenth Path of
the Tree of Life, the Illuminating Intelligence, so named because it is
"that Channel of Scintillating Flame which is the founder of the
concealed and fundamental ideas of holiness and of their stages of
preparation." This is the Path of Fire, of Judgement and of
Resurrection. It is the Path of the Ascension of the Lord Jesus Christ
and the Path of the Descent of the Holy Ghost. It is Jacob's Ladder
with Angels ascending and descending. Here is Osiris ascending to
Kether; the Hindu Akasa and Agni; the Greek Iacchus as Lord of
Ecstasy, the Roman Bacchus; Horus, Pluto and Vulcan as gods of
Fire. I honor the Great Ones of this Path and like them, I would walk
the Shining Way to Illumination.*

Stand. Remove girdle and robe. The rest of the Rite is to be performed
naked. Go deosil to south, make Circled Cross with right forefinger
over incense, saying:

Be blessed by the Great Ones in whose honor you shall burn.

Cast incense into Censer, saying:

May Michael's spear from there to here make the Magic Fire appear.

Cense Altar, saying:

> *Lord of Fire!*
> *Lord of Light!*
> *Lord of Ecstasy!*

Replace Censer. Make Sign of Fire: Raise both hands to forehead,
palms outward, thumbs along line of eyebrows, tips touching. Tips of
forefingers touching. Thus you make an upward pointing triangle on
your forehead which is the Sign of Fire. Arms returned to side, go to
west. Make L. V. X. Signs. Then say:

> *Holy art Thou, Lord of the Universe!*
> *Holy art Thou, whom nature hath not formed.*
> *Holy art Thou, the vast and the mighty One.*
> *Lord of the light and of the darkness.*

*Praise be to thee, oh Lord, King of Eternal Glory! Let me adore the
Lord, for it is he who made me. For the Lord is a great God, and a
great king above all gods, Kether is his abode and Eheieh is his Name.
In his hands are the depths of the sea, and the tops of the mountains*

are his. For it is he who made us. His is the sea, for he made it, and the dry land, which his hands have formed. [Kneel.] Let me bow down in worship, let me kneel before the Lord who made me. [Rise.] For he is my God, I am of the people he shepherds, of the flock he guides. I praise the Lord, for it is he who made me. [Cover or close the eyes.] Hear, O Israel; the Lord is our God, the Lord is One. Blessed be his name, whose glorious kingdom is for ever and ever. [Uncover or open the eyes.] And thou shalt love the Lord thy God with all thine heart, and with all thy soul, and with all thy might. [Pause.] O, my God! I love thee above all things, with my whole heart and soul, because thou art all-good and worthy of all my love. [Pause.] God is love; and he that abideth in love, abideth in God. God is Light; and if we walk in the light we have fellowship one with another. God is Spirit; and they that worship him must worship him in spirit and in truth. It is the Spirit that beareth witness; because the Spirit is Truth. Beyond Kether are the three Veils of the Unmanifest; and those three are one. There are three that bear record in heaven, the Father, the Word, and the Holy Spirit, and these three are One. The Supreme Unity is of three degrees or natures. IAO! IAO! IAO! God the three in one. One in three and three in one. Kether! Chokmah! Binah! There are three that bear witness on earth, the water, the blood, and the tears, and these three agree in one. Glory be to the Father and to the Son and to the Holy Spirit; as it was in the beginning, is now, and ever shall be, world without end. Amen.

Dance deosil around Altar three times, singing or saying:

> *One day when heaven was filled with his praises,*
> *One day when sin was black as could be,*
> *Jesus came forth to be born of a virgin,*
> *Lived, loved and laboured—my leader is he.*

> *One day they led him up Calvary's mountain,*
> *One day they nailed him for me on the tree;*
> *Wonderful, Counsellor, they had acclaimed him,*
> *Now he is leader—my leader is he.*

> *One day when fullness of time was fast dawning,*
> *One day the stone moved away from the door,*
> *Then he arose, over death he had conquered,*
> *Now he's ascended—my Lord evermore.*

Return to west, continue:

> *One day he's coming, for him I am longing;*
> *One day the skies with his glory will shine;*
> *Wonderful day, my beloved ones bringing;*
> *Hope of the hopeless, this Jesus is mine.*

Then say:

> *Lord, as Krishna, thou hast said—*
> *I am the birthless, the deathless,*
> *   Lord of all that breathes.*
> *I seem to be born;*
> *It is only seeming.*
> *When goodness grows weak,*
> *   When evil increases,*
> *I make myself a body.*
> *In every age I come back*
> *   To deliver the holy,*
> *To destroy the sin of the sinner,*
> *To establish righteousness.*

Dark are the days and darker are the nights, O Lord. I look to the east for the dawning of thy light.

Salute the east. Say:

> *Come Horus! Crowned and conquering!*
> *Come Apollo! Dispelling the night.*
> *Lord Maitreya! We await thy dawning;*
> *Heru-ra-ha, Lord of the Light!*

> *But whatever name thou comest;*
> *Bless us who pray this night:*
> *Thou Christ who comest in glory,*
> *Lord Jesus, thou King of the Light!*

Therefore with Angels and Archangels, with Thrones, Dominions, Princedoms, Virtues, Powers, with Kerubim and Seraphim, and all the company of heaven, I laud and magnify thy glorious name, evermore praising thee and saying: Holy, holy, holy, Lord God of Hosts, heaven and earth are full of thy glory; glory be to thee, O Lord most high.

Perform the Qabalistic Cross. Sit. Enter the Silence. After a while, stand and sing or say:

> *O Lord my God! When I in awesome wonder*
> *Consider all the worlds thy hands have made,*
> *I see the stars, I hear the rolling thunder,*
> *Thy pow'r throughout the universe displayed—* ·

> *Then sings my soul, my saviour God to thee;*
> *How great thou art, how great thou art!*
> *Then sings my soul, my saviour God to thee;*
> *How great thou art, how great thou art!*

> *When through the woods and forest glades I wander*
> *And hear the birds sing sweetly in the trees;*
> *When I look down from lofty mountain grandeur*
> *And hear the brook and feel the gentle breeze;*

> *Then sings my soul, my saviour God to thee;*
> *How great thou art, how great thou art!*
> *Then sings my soul, my saviour God to thee;*
> *How great thou art, how great thou art!*

O Lord of the Universe! Grant thou that upon me may shine forth the light of my Higher Soul. Let me be guided by the light of mine own Holy Guardian Angel unto thy throne of glory, ineffable in the center of the Cosmos of Life and Light. May the influence of the Divine Ones descend upon my head, and teach me the value of self-sacrifice so that I shrink not in the hour of trial; but that my Genius may stand in the presence of the Holy One in that hour when the Son of Man is evoked before the Lord of Spirits and his name in the presence of the Ancient of Days.

Visualize the Higher Self (an idealized picture of a youthful but mature you that is perfect in every way) standing in the distant east. Raise right arm to an angle of forty-five degrees in greeting and say:

Adoration unto thee that dawnest in the golden! O thou that sailest over the heavens in thy bark of morning! Dark before thee is the golden brightness; in whom are all the hues of the rainbow! [Lower arm.] May I walk as thou walkest, O holiness who has no master. Thou art the great space-wanderer in whom hundreds of thousands of years are as but one moment. Let me enter with thee into thy bark;

let me pass with thee as thou enterest the Gate of the West where
thou gleamest in the gloaming as thy mother Binah enfoldeth thee!

Go deosil around Altar, saying:

*Dark is all the world, without, within. There is light alone in thee, O
Glory of the Godhead Unspeakable! Eternal Master! Ancient of
Days! Thee, thee I invoke in my need! Rend asunder, tear aside the
Veil of the Sanctuary and let mine eyes behold my Holy Guardian
Angel! As it is written; the lightning lighteneth in the east and flasheth
even unto the west, even so shall be the coming of the Son of Man.*

Stop in west and say:

*I am come forth from the Gates of Darkness! Behold, I am come to
the gate of the Shining Ones of Heaven, I stand between the mighty
pillars of that gate! Open, open unto me, O Gate of the God of Light!*

Again visualize the Higher Self, but this time much nearer. Say:

*Come forth, come forth, mine own Higher Self, my Buddhic Self, my
Christ Self; come unto me thou that art crowned with starlight; thou
that shinest amongst the Lords of Truth; whose place is in the abode
of the Spirits of Heaven!*

Exalt unto the Higher Self. Imagine it as encompassing you and
entering into you as a blazing light. Say:

*I am the resurrection and the life. I am he that liveth but was dead,
and behold I am alive for evermore. I have passed through the Gates
of Darkness unto Light! I am a lord of life, triumphant over death.
There is no part of me that is not of the gods!* [Pause.] *Let the
brilliance of the Divine Light descend!*

Cross arms on breast, finger touching opposite shoulders, head
thrown back, eyes closed. Long pause. Afterward, kneel and say:

*Adoration be unto thee, Lord of my life, for thou hast permitted me to
enter thus far into the sanctuary of thine ineffable mystery, and hast
vouchsafed to manifest unto me some little fragment of the glory of
thy being.*

Arise, take Cup, offer it and say:

*And before thee I do promise and vow; that with the aid of the Great
Ones, I will so purify my heart and mind that I may one day become*

truly and wholly united unto thee who art in truth my higher Genius, my Master, my Guide, my Holy Guardian Angel, mine own Divine Self! For I know that my redeemer liveth, and that he shall stand at the latter day upon the earth.

Drink, replace Cup. Salute the Altar and give Sign of Silence. The Rite is finished.

CORRESPONDENCES OF PATH THIRTEEN

Element of Fire. The elemental beings are the Salamanders, the spirits of Fire. The Hebrew letter is Shin which means Tooth and represents Spirit. Tarot Atu XX, Judgement, the secret title of which is "the Spirit of the Primal Fire." Esoteric message of Tarot Atu XX is "Resurrection is hidden in Death." Its divinatory significance is "final decision in respect of the past, a new current in respect of the future; always represents the taking of a definite step, upright good, reversed doubtful to bad." The card's instruction in Magic: "Be every act an act of love and worship. Be every act the Fiat of God. Be every act a source of radiant glory!"

Rosary-Novena to the Lady

Required reading: *The Gospel According to St. John.* Read it aloud either before beginning the Novena or during the nine-day period.

Time: Begin the Novena when waxing Moon is in a Water Sign, continue nightly for nine nights.

PART ONE

On Altar are Tarot Atu XII, the Hanged Man, a Roman Catholic Rosary, Cup with Water, and three tall white candles. Black Pillar in northeast corner of room, white Pillar in southwest corner. Ritual Book on stand by chair in west. Incense: myrrh. Robed, girded and sandaled, enter, salute Altar, go deosil lighting candles and igniting charcoal, go to west, sit. Read aloud:

The Twelfth Path of the Tree of Life is "the Intelligence of Transparency because it is that species of Magnificence called

Seership, which is named the place whence issues the vision of those seeing apparitions, that is, the place whence issue the prophecies made by seers." Path Twelve connects Kether and Binah. To it is assigned the Hebrew letter Mem which means Water and has the numerical value of 40, Tarot Atu XII, the Hanged Man, and the Element Water. The elemental beings of this Path are the Undines or Nymphs, the Spirits of Water. May I be flexible and attentive to images as are the Undines, yet may I avoid idleness and change- ability. May I be as receptive and sensitive as the Spirits of Water and as fluidic and germinative as they.

Stand. Make Sign of Water: Place both open hands downward flat against stomach or solar plexus, thumbs along line of diaphragm, tips touching. Fingers extended, tips of forefingers touching. Thus you make a downward pointing triangle which is the Sign of Water. Say:

O glorious Gabriel, Archangel of Water, lend me, I pray, thy powerful aid.

Go deosil to south, put incense in Censer and cense Altar, saying:

> *Hail Rhea! Goddess who flows!*
> *Hail Isis! Lady of Water!*
> *Hail Gabriel! Potent of God!*

Replace Censer. Go to west, take Tarot card, hold it high and say:

Redeemer in the Waters! Bearer of the Great Secret! Reveal to me your Mystery! [Lower card and gaze at it for a moment.] *The Hanged Man! From a gallows shaped like the letter T hangs by one foot a fair young man. His other leg forms a cross with the suspended one. His hands are behind his back, perhaps tied. His mouth is resolutely closed. A golden halo is around his head. The mystic title is "Redeemer in the Waters." The redeemer is the Holy One, the Son of God, the Christ Within, the Buddhic Self, the I Am Self. The esoteric message is "the Secret is hidden between the waters that are above and the waters that are beneath." The waters that are above is Binah. The waters that are beneath is Malkuth. Suspended between Binah and Malkuth is the Secret. But what is the secret? Path Twelve is the passage between Kether and Binah. Kether is Pure Divinity.*

Binah is the Motherhood of God. The Holy One is suspended in the Amniotic Waters of the Great Mother awaiting his birth, waiting to be transported via the Chariot to Tiphareth, from there to go by the paths of the Sun and the Moon to the Earth. His secret is what he carries with him and he carries that which is his source, the pure divinity of Kether. A messenger of the Gods has asked, "Know ye not that ye are Gods?" And another has said, "Sole root of fault, O man, in thee, is not to know thine own divinity." The secret then is— inherent divinity! The Son of God voluntarily sacrifices his unlimited divinity to be incarnated so as to bring his humanhood up to his godhood! [Pause for reflection.] The divinatory significance of this Atu is sacrifice. If the card is upright the sacrifice is voluntary, if upside-down the sacrifice is imposed by circumstances of environment and karma. In either case suffering is entailed. Whether the suffering ennobles or degrades depends upon other factors, including the will of the sufferer. [Pause to understand and memorize.] The theurgic instruction of the Hanged Man is [again elevate card] "Let not the waters whereon thou journeyest wet thee. And, being come to shore, plant thou the vine and rejoice without shame." [Lower card.] This is a direct allusion to the Dionysian Mysteries which sought to find realization of divinity through inducing states of ecstacy. This I also seek.

Replace card. Sit. Read aloud:

> In the castle of my soul
> Is a little postern gate,
> Whereat, when I enter,
> I am in the presence of God.
> In a moment, in the turning of a thought,
> I am where God is,
> This is a fact.
>
> When I enter into God,
> All life has meaning,
> Without asking I know;
> My desires are even now fulfilled,
> My fever is gone
> In the great quiet of God.
> My troubles are but pebbles on the road,
> My joys are like the everlasting hills.

*So it is when my soul steps through the postern gate
Into the presence of God,
Big things become small and small things become great.
The near becomes far, and the future is near.
The lowly and despised is shot through with glory...
God is the substance of all revolutions;
When I am in God, I am in the Kingdom of Heaven,
And in the Motherland of my Soul.*

Close your eyes and visualize your own postern gate. Enter the Silence and go through your postern gate. Afterward, say:

Praise be to thee, O Holy Mother!

PART TWO

Seated in the west with stand before you on which is Cup with water, say:

To this Twelfth Path of the Tree of Life is assigned the Element of Water. Water is before me. This Path is called the place whence issues the vision of those seeing apparitions, that is, the place whence issue the prophecies made by seers. Great Mother, Great Mother, Great Mother dear! Permit me, I pray, to become a seer!

Lean forward, rest elbows on stand, thumb between forefinger and middle finger of clenched hands, cheekbones resting on ball or heel of hands, gaze into the water of the Cup, willing the inner vision to unfold. Enter the Silence. Afterward, say:

Praise be to thee, O Holy Mother!

PART THREE

Hold the cross of the Rosary in the right hand and perform the Qabalistic Cross. Still holding the cross say:

I believe in the Father-Mother-hood of God, the brotherhood of all life everywhere, the leadership of the Great Elder Brothers of Mankind including the Lord Jesus Christ, salvation by character, and the progession of man upward and onward forever.

On the first large bead after the cross say:

Our Father, who art in heaven: Hallowed be thy Name. Thy Kingdom come, thy will be done in earth as it is in heaven. Give us this day our daily bread; and forgive us our trespasses as we forgive those who trespass against us; and let us not be led into temptation but deliver us from evil.

On each of the next three small beads, say:

Hail Mary, full of grace! The Lord is with thee: blessed art thou amongst women, and blessed is the fruit of thy womb, Jesus. Glory be to the Father and to the Son and to the Holy Spirit; As it was in the beginning, is now and ever shall be, world without end. Amen.

Then say:

The first triad of the Holy Rosary, the five Joyful Mysteries. The first Joyful Mystery, the Annunciation.

Meditate: Contemplate in this Mystery how the Archangel Gabriel saluted the Blessed Lady with the title, "full of grace," and announced unto her the incarnation of the Son of God. Pray for the virtue and grace of voluntary sacrifice in imitation of him. While meditating on each Mystery say the Our Father on the large bead just before the medal and the Hail Mary on each of the next ten small beads after the medal; adding after the tenth Hail Mary, the Glory be to the Father. Then say:

The second Joyful Mystery, the Visitation.

Meditate: Contemplate in this Mystery how the Blessed Virgin Mary, understanding from the angel that her cousin Elizabeth had conceived, went with haste into the mountains of Judea to visit her, and remained with her three months. Ask through the intercession of our Lady the grace of perfect charity toward our neighbor. Then say:

The third Joyful Mystery, the Nativity.

Meditate: Contemplate in this Mystery how the Blessed Virgin Mary, when the time of her delivery was come, brought forth her child, Christ Jesus, at midnight in a cave below the cavern, on the third day she brought him forth and laid him in a manger, because there was no room for him in the inns of Bethlehem. Ask to have revealed to you the Great Mystery of the Incarnation of God in human form, and seek to understand it, not by intellect and reason, but by love and in faith. Then say:

The fourth Joyful Mystery, the Presentation.

Meditate: Contemplate in this Mystery how the Blessed Mother, on the day of her purification, presented the child Jesus in the Temple, where holy Simeon, giving thanks to God with great devotion, received the baby into his arms. Like Mary, who was submissive to the Jewish law, we should cultivate the virtue of obedience. Then say:

The fifth Joyful Mystery, the Finding in the Temple.

Meditate: Contemplate in this Mystery how Mary, having lost her beloved son in Jerusalem, sought him for the space of three days, and at length found him in the Temple in the midst of the doctors, discoursing learnedly with them, being then but twelve years old. Ask that you too, after spiritual childhood, may be about your Father's business. Finally say:

Hail, Holy Queen of Angels, our sweetness and our hope! Praise be to thee, O Holy Mother!

PART FOUR

Temple arranged as in Part One, with fresh candles, charcoal and incense, and fresh water in cup. Enter, salute Altar, go deosil lighting candles and igniting charcoal, go to west, sit. Read aloud:

Dionysus, god of ecstacy and joy, god of laughter, spirit of revel and rapture, was son of Zeus. His mortal mother was Semele, daughter of Cadmus, founder and king of the city of Thebes in Greece. Dionysus

was delivered from his mother's womb by the fire of a lightning-flash
which killed her. Semele's jealous sisters said that Dionysus was not
the progeny of Zeus but that she, being with child by some mortal,
ascribed to Zeus the loss of her virginity. They loudly insisted that this
lie about the father of her child was the sin for which Zeus had struck
her dead.

> But when on the womb that held him
> The fire-bolt flew from the hand of Zeus;
> And pains of child-birth bound his mother fast,
> And she cast him forth untimely,
> And under the lightning's lash relinquished life;
> Then Zeus the son of Kronos
> Ensconsed him instantly in a secret womb
> Chambered within his thigh,
> And with gold pins closed him.

> So, when the Fates had made him ripe for birth,
> Zeus bore the bull-horned god.
> The god, child of god,
> Spirit of revel and rapture, Dionysus!

Stand, go deosil to south, put incense into Censer and cense Altar,
saying:

> Io, Io, Bacchus!
> Io, Io, God of Joy!
> Io, Io, Kybele, Mother of us all!

Replace Censer saying:

May the air be thick with scent of Myrrh!

Go to west, sit. Read aloud:

Semele's sisters declared she was lying when she said she was
pregnant by Zeus. Isis became pregnant with Harpocrates after her
husband Osiris' death, and Set spread the rumor she was lying about
the father of her child. Joseph married Mary during her pregnancy
and to this day people doubt her story that she was still virgin though

pregnant. In Theurgy a Mystery is something that from an everyday common-sense point of view is either quite impossible, obviously untrue or highly unlikely, but from another point of view, that of occultism, need not necessarily be historically or literally true but nevertheless is spiritually, cosmically and eternally true. Such stories as the virgin birth of the saviour gods of many religions belong to this category, including the story of the birth of Jesus Christ. Most orthodox Christians believe and affirm that Jesus was and is unique in human history. But he was not. Rama, Krishna, Orpheus, Hermes, Mithras and others have stories similar to that of Jesus, in fact the Ageless Wisdom reveals that they all were Avatars, human incarnations of God the Son, the Cosmic Christ, the Solar Logos. And the old gods still exist, for they are but names given by various peoples to the many manifestations and offices of the Eternal One. In the interstices of time and space, in the folds of the warp and woof of universal consciousness, in the deeps of the collective unconscious, the Great Ones exist eternally—and can be called forth.

Stand. Dance deosil around Altar, singing or saying:

> *Great Mother, Great Mother, Great Mother of all;*
> *Give heed, dear Mother, give heed as I call.*
> *Demeter, Kybele, Hertha; give aid!*
> *For thee I call, O Mother, O Maid!*
> *Many-named matron, bitter and sweet,*
> *Terrible and beautiful from head to feet;*
> *I fear you, I love you, I need you to be*
> *Watchful and guiding, ever near unto me.*
>
> *Protect me, inspire me, teach me to know*
> *The way to maturity that I am to go.*
> *Lovely Lady, Lovely lady, lovely Lady of Light,*
> *Come dance with me, dance with me, dance, dance, tonight.*

Whirling, jumping, laughing, laughing, laughing, dance until you fall exhausted. Then stand, take Cup, offer it, saying:

Praise be to thee, O Holy Mother!

Drink, replace Cup. Salute Altar and give Sign of Silence.

PART FIVE

Seated to the west, read aloud:

There is an aspect of the Great Mother that needs to be assimilated: Ama, the dark sterile mother, Nephthys, the dark mother. She is the troubled one, the disturbed one, sometimes the selfish and thoughtless one, sometimes neglectful and cruel. She is to be pitied and understood—and loved.

Go to the north and crouch there. Identify with the bewildered, neglected child. Feel the child whimpering. Read aloud:

Mommy! It's dark and I'm afraid. Mommy, where are you? I hurt and I need you. Mommy, I'm scared. Please come to me, mommy, please, please, please! And please don't hurt me. Like you did. You know. I don't mind it when you scold me like you used to. Remember, mommy? Or even spank me, even if I cry, because then I know you love me. We had lots of good times, didn't we mommy? It was fun, wasn't it? But don't go away from me, mommy, please don't leave me. Don't stay away, mommy, please come back. Even if it is with one of them. I can hear you sometimes, when you're with one of them, laughing and laughing. And I'm glad for you mommy, I'm glad you're having a good time, even if you make me stay out. But sometimes you cry. And he makes funny noises. Is he hurting you, mommy? I hate him! I hate him! I hate him! and sometimes I even hate you, mommy. Like now. I hate you! I hate you! I hate you! But I love you too. Please come back, mommy, I want you. I'm scared mommy. Please come back, please!

Comfort the frightened child. Understand and forgive the neglectful mother.

PART SIX

Hold the cross of the Rosary in the right hand and perform the Qabalistic Cross (see page 144). Then continue the same procedure and ending as in Part Three (see page 146).

The middle part is the second triad of the Holy Rosary, the five Sorrowful Mysteries. The first Sorrowful Mystery, the Prayer and Bloody Sweat of Jesus in the Garden.

Meditate: Contemplate in this Mystery how Jesus was so afflicted for mankind in the Garden of Gethsemane that his body was bathed in a bloody sweat which ran trickling down in great drops upon the ground. Ask that we may sincerely lament our sins which caused this great agony. Then say:

The second Sorrowful Mystery, the Scourging of Jesus at the Pillar.

Meditate: Contemplate in this Mystery how Jesus was most cruelly scourged in Pilate's house. Let us ask for the courage to speak out against cruelty to the innocent. Then say:

The third Sorrowful Mystery, the Crowning of Jesus with Thorns.

Meditate: Contemplate in this Mystery how Jesus was cruelly crowned with sharp thorns and saluted with derision as King of the Jews. Let us fly the vanities and flatteries of this world and seek only the approval of God. Then say:

The fourth Sorrowful Mystery, Jesus Carries his Cross.

Meditate: Contemplate in this Mystery how Jesus, being sentenced to die, bore with great patience the cross which was laid upon him for his greater torment and ignominy. In bearing the crosses and trials of life we should remember this Mystery and try to imitate the wonderful patience which Jesus displayed. Then say:

The fifth Sorrowful Mystery, the Crucifixion.

Meditate. Contemplate in this Mystery how Jesus being come to Mount Calvary, was stripped of his clothes, and his hands and feet most cruelly nailed to the cross. As he prayed for his executioners, so let us forgive those who injure and persecute us.

PART SEVEN

Temple arranged as in Part I with fresh water in Cup, fresh candles, charcoal, incense. Bowls of water on floor in east and west. Robed, girded and sandaled, enter and perform Opening Exercises of Temple Rite, censing the Altar after the Sign of the Enterer. Go deosil to the east, make invoking Pentagram of Water toward the west and say:

Elohim Tzabaoth! Elohim of Hosts! Glory be to the Ruach Elohim who moved upon the face of the waters of creation.

Make Sign of Water. Say:

In the Name of Elohim Tzabaoth, I evoke the Undines, the Spirits of Water!

Take Cup in both hands and with it make large Circled Cross in the air toward the west and say:

Come, little ones of Water, come! You are welcome!

Kiss Cup and say:

Fount of Life, Vehicle of the Spirit, Womb of the Mother, Bringer Forth of Form—we love you!

Replace Cup. Dance deosil around Altar, dipping fingers in the bowls of water and flinging drops into the air. Sing:

Un-dines, won't you dance with me?
Come dance with me, O dance with me.
Un-dines, won't you dance with me?
O dance with me tonight.
Round and round and round we go,
And where we go the waters flow!
Un-dines, won't you dance with me?
O dance with me tonight.

Return to east, say:

Let us rehearse the Prayer of the Undines.

Kneel in east, facing west. Immerse left hand in bowl of water as you read:

Terrible King of the Sea! Thou who holdest the keys of the Cataracts of Heaven and who encloseth the subterranean Waters in the cavernous hollows of earth; King of the Deluge and the Rains of Spring; thou who openest the sources of the rivers and of the fountains, thou who commandest Moisture which is the Blood of the Earth to become the sap of the plants; we adore thee and we serve thee! Speak unto us in the murmur of the Limpid Waters and we shall desire thy love! O Vastness wherein all the Rivers of Being seek to lose themselves and which renew themselves ever in thee! O thou Ocean of Infinite Perfection! O Height which reflecteth thyself in the Depth! O Depth which exalteth thyself unto the Height! Lead us into the true life through intelligence and through love! Lead us into immortality through sacrifice, that we may be found worthy to offer one day unto you, the Water, the Blood and the Tears. So mote it be, So mote it be.

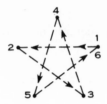

Pause for psychical attunement. Then rise and make banishing Pentagram of Water toward the west. Say:

Little Messengers of Water, depart ye in peace unto your habitations. May the blessing of Elohim Tzabaoth be upon you. Be there peace between you and me, and be you ready to come when you are called.

Go deosil to west, take Cup, offer it, saying:

Elohim Tzabaoth!

Drink, replace Cup, sit. Perform Closing Exercises of Temple Rite.

PART EIGHT

Statue or picture of Madonna and Child in the west with candles on either side. Kneel before it and say:

Mother of divine grace,
Mother most pure
Mother most chaste,
Mother inviolate,
Mother undefiled,
Mother most amiable,
Mother of good counsel,
Mother of our Lord, Bless me!

Virgin most prudent,
Virgin most venerable,
Virgin most renowned,
Virgin most powerful,
Virgin most merciful,
Virgin most faithful, bless me!

Cause of our joy,
Spiritual vessel,
Vessel of honor,
Singular vessel of devotion,
Mystical rose,
Ark of the covenant,
Gate of heaven,
Morning Star,
Health of the weak,
Refuge of the lost,
Comfort of the afflicted,
Help of the helpless, bless me!

Queen of angels,
Queen of patriarchs,
Queen of prophets,
Queen of apostles,
Queen of disciples,
Queen of martyrs,
Queen of virgins,
Queen of all saints,
Queen of the Holy Rosary,
Queen of peace, bless me!

Enter the Silence. Afterward say:

Praise be to thee, O Holy Mother!

PART NINE

Hold the cross of the Rosary in the right hand and perform the Qabalistic Cross as discussed on page 144. Then continue the same procedure and ending as in Part Three on page 146. The middle part is:

The third triad of the Holy Rosary, the five Glorious Mysteries. The first Glorious Mystery, the Resurrection.

Meditate: Contemplate how the Lord Jesus Christ, triumphing gloriously over death, rose again the third day. Give thanks to Almighty God that so do we all. Then say:

The second Glorious Mystery, the Ascension.

Meditate: Contemplate how the Lord Jesus Christ, forty days after his resurrection, ascended unto heaven, attended by angels, and in the sight of his mother and his apostles and disciples. Feel an ardent longing for heaven, our true home. Then say:

The Third Glorious Mystery, the Descent of the Holy Spirit.

Meditate: Contemplate how our Lord sent, as he promised, the Holy Spirit upon his apostles, who, after he ascended, returning to Jerusalem, continued in prayer and supplication, expecting the fullfillment of his promise. May the Holy Spirit descend also upon us bringing the Gifts of the Spirit. Then say:

The fourth Glorious Mystery, the Assumption.

Meditate: Contemplate the legend of how the Virgin Mary, some years after the resurrection of her son, passed out of this world unto him, and was by him assumed into heaven, signifying the return of the Mother to Binah. Let us accept her as a personification of the Mother aspect of Divinity. Then say:

The fifth Glorious Mystery, the Crowning of the Blessed Virgin.

Meditate: Contemplate the Virgin Mary being crowned by her son as Queen of Heaven, signifying the glory of the Three Supernals. Finally say:

Hail, Holy Queen of Angels, our sweetness and our hope! Praise be to thee, O Holy Mother!

Rite of Path Eleven

The Fool of God

THE FOOL

The Theurgist should collect material, write, memorize, rehearse and perform his own individual Rite of Path Eleven, making use of his originality and creativity but remaining true to the basic symbolism of the Path as expressed in the following:

Element: Air.

Time: Waxing Moon in an Air Sign. Or perhaps April Fool's Day or Shrove Tuesday. An early dawn on a Spring day.

Tools: The four Instruments. In their proper places or perhaps in a pouch attached to a pole as with the Fool of the Tarot. Cup empty (full of Air). Perhaps added symbols to emphasize Air, such as fan, butterfly, etc.

Flowers: Roses.

Incense: That of Air. Galbanum if possible, otherwise rose petals.

Clothing: Robed as usual or sky-clad or special costume such as that of the Fool or of a clown.

Suggested Music: Nonsense songs or children's songs.

Bible Reading: Before the Rite, the *Gospel According to St. Matthew.* During the Rite, *First Corinthians,* Chapter 1, verses 8 to 31.

Hebrew Letter: ALEPH, Ox.

Sephirotic Text: "The Eleventh Path is the Scintillating Intelligence because it is the essence of that curtain which is place closed to the order of the disposition, and this is a speical dignity given to it that it may be able to stand before the face of the Cause of Causes."

Tarot Atu: 0. The Fool. Le Mat. The Holy Innocent. Spirit of Aether. In Divination the Fool signifies an original, subtle, sudden impulse coming from a completely strange quarter; idea, thought, inspiration; reversed it means folly, eccentricity. Its Magic Message is: "Know naught! All ways are lawful to innocence. Pure folly is the key to Initiation. Silence breaks into Rapture. Be neither man nor woman, but both in one. Be silent, Babe in the Egg of Blue, that thou mayest grow to bear the Lance and Graal! Wander alone and sing! In the king's palace his daughter awaits thee."

Elementals: The Sylphs, Spirits of Air.

Magical Power: Divination especially in the deeper meaning of word; "to divine."

Psychic Sense: Clairaudience.

Suggestions for research: find ideas, quotations, themes. Setting: the breath of God; the Holy Ghost; the Holy Spirit; the Holy Innocent; Harpocrates; Hoor-Par-Krat; Bacchus Diphues; Der reine Thor; the Pure Fool; Parsifal; Percivale of the Round Table; the Green Man of Spring; the medieval Court Jester; Harlequinade of the Commedia dell'Arte; Punch and Judy; I Pagliacci; Dostoevsky's *The Idiot.*

RECOMMENDED READING

The Mystical Qabalah, by Dion Fortune
Kabbalah, Tradition of Hidden Knowledge,
  by Z'ev ben Shimon Halevi
Holy Kabbalah: A Study of the Secret Tradition, by A.E. Waite
The Kybalion, by Three Initiates
Mysticism, by Evelyn Underhill
The Hero with a Thousand Faces, by Joseph Campbell
The Occult, a History, by Colin Wilson
The Psychology of C. G. Jung, by Jolande Jacobi
Occult Psychology, by Alta J. LaDage
The Tree of Life, by Israel Regardie

 Clifford Bias was a well-known teacher in New York City. He lived at the Ansonia Hotel on the West Side, and taught tarot classes, the kabbalah, the Western Mystery Tradition, as well as classes in spiritualism and psychic development. Lots of people knew him as a teacher; even more know him because they went to the Ansonia for a reading. Bias lived in New York until 1985, when he moved to Indiana as education director and president of the Indiana Association of Spiritualists in Camp Chesterfield.

Reverend Bias was ordained as a minister in 1937, and helped organize the Spiritualist-Episcopal Church. He served as a minister at churches in Jackson, MI; Buffalo, NY; Toledo, OH; St. Petersburg, FL; and New York City. He helped found the Universal Spiritualist Association, for which he was a dean.

He compiled and edited *The Ritual Book of Magic*, published by Weiser in 1981. He left this plane in 1987 at the age of 77. He had a vast background in the field of esoteric study. There are many who will miss him. This work has been offered again for those students who want to have one last chance to study with Clifford.